I've Never Had a Bad Day

The 5 Cornerstone Choices to Help You Build Your Best Life

I hope you enjoy reading my book!
my dear family, Matthew Pena
Blessings to you and your family!

Waleed Soro 1-10-2023

ISBN 978-1-939237-91-0

Published by Suncoast Digital Press, Inc.
Sarasota, Florida, U.S.A.

DEDICATED TO
MY MOTHER AND FATHER

Siham Daoud Soro   Yousif Toma Soro

CONTENTS

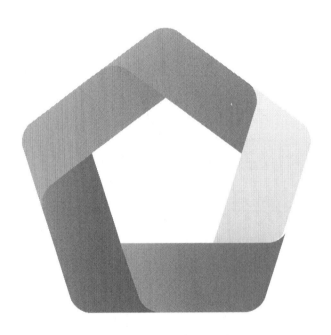

PREFACE

I've never had a bad day in my life. And you can have this too!

I grew up very poor in Iraq. As children, our soccer ball was a collection of scraps and rags tied together into a round shape.

But even as a child, I knew I had a choice about how my day would go, and that's when I started knowing, really knowing, that I could choose to live so that I can honestly say, "I've never had a bad day in my life."

At 10 years old, my family and I were watching our tiny little black and white television. It was a movie starring Clark Gable and Marilyn Monroe. I said to my dad, "Wow, she is so beautiful. I am going to marry my own Marilyn some day."

He laughed and said, "Okay, well, there isn't even one blonde anywhere around here, but good luck with that."

Life went on. I made my choices which affirmed myself, my confidence, and my positive attitude every single day.

I was 19 when I came to America. To Detroit.

I had no command of English. I mean none. I wanted to make new friends, so I went to a disco.

I was stunned—amazed! So many beautiful people having fun dancing disco!

I knew what to do.

I got a job, bought John Travolta clothes and got a John Travolta haircut.

At the club, I watched the feet and memorized the disco movements. I went home and practiced. I loved dancing at the club because not only was it exciting, it did not matter that my English was so poor—dance is its own language.

I went to dance contests and it was so much fun! Within six months I was the Michigan State Champion! True story!

I was celebrating with everyone at the club, having so much fun dancing disco to American music…and in walks the girl of my dreams. Yes, I ended up meeting my own beautiful "Marilyn"—and we've been married 42 years!

In the years since my disco days, I have enjoyed much success in the food manufacturing business, where I started and built a national brand. I've moved around, had wonderful adventures, and raised a beautiful family, all by following my heart.

What I want for everyone is to understand how to stay connected to their heart, live true to themselves, and <u>never have a bad day.</u>

Our potential to have a good day is determined not by our circumstances, but rather by our choices, our intention to make it so.

This book will take the mystery out of this possibility—this opportunity that you have to be able to have only good days. **There are five things to focus on in order to build your best life.** These five choices that I have the pleasure to share with you are from my personal life experiences. From my childhood until this present moment!

The **clarity** you can gain from making **The Five Cornerstone Choices** that you will learn in this book will empower you in every aspect of your life: your actions will begin to more and more automatically align with your choices. Life gets easier.

The purpose of this book is to help you claim your power of choice and live a life that you love. No matter what age, each of us faces challenges every day. My intention in writing this book is to help you embrace and resolve each of your challenges more easily than you now think is possible.

Does "Easier" Mean Settling for Less Successful?

Many of my speaking audience members are between 25 and 35 years old and you, my valued reader of my first book, may also be a young adult. The pressure of "potential" is never more forceful than when you are at this rapidly blossoming stage of life. Many feel a frenetic need to decide on a career, get a job, move out from under the protection of their parents, make money, and be successful quickly. In this chapter of life, you hear from multiple sources that it is time to focus on reaching your full potential.

Full human potential. Isn't it interesting that no one knows how to define that, how to quantify it, much less how to achieve it? We have a sense that it is vast and that some people reach further into its mysterious depths than others. We realize that we each have the potential to live more fully; that in our own lives, each area can expand and improve.

Whether you believe that we are human beings seeking an enlightened experience, or that we are spiritual beings having a human experience, the fact is that each day is a gift to open and enjoy, knowing that our quantity of days is limited, but how we fill them doesn't need to be. It is completely up to us to have one quality day follow another.

Ever since a profound experience that I remember even though I was only five years old, I have chosen to live my life this way—one quality day following another. Now, many decades later, the truth is that **I have never had a bad day**.

I have lived from a place of choice to never have a bad day, overcoming some extreme and serious challenges and navigating a life journey across the globe. I built from scratch a business enterprise that produced great wealth for me and my family. The purpose of sharing my life story in the chapters ahead is to show **how my choices played out** and to confirm to you that now is the very best time in your life to make the critical, high-level choices that put you in the driver's seat of your life.

The Power of Choice

The power of choice is the primary tool that you have at your disposal to impact your life by effecting change. Considering that change is intrinsic to each moment, there is no avoiding it. You can say, "Wow, this is perfect" when you are experiencing something wonderful that life has offered you—yet, that moment changes to the next—and "this" is gone and in the *past* before you can say "perfect." But, in the elegant and awesome design of being human, every moment is an opportunity to live from a place of choice; your future is dependent upon the choices and decisions you make.

Over the last two years, I have immersed myself in the task of distilling down what I've learned, what has proven to work (not just for me, but for anyone) to be able to say, "I've never had a bad day." Now, with this book, I can share the cornerstones, the principles that you need to build your own version of a life full of positivity and joy.

In **Part One**, you'll discover the five life choices which support those cornerstones. You'll see for yourself the benefits of making each choice. My purpose in sharing them with you is to give you access to their power. These are tools to use—not just ideas to contemplate.

In **Part Three** you will find helpful, concrete support for applying the principles presented in this book. Part Three is all about practical application: Resources, inspirational coaching, introductions to other experts, recommended action steps, suggested excellent books, and helpful exercises for you to actually take time to complete.

What's in the second part, the middle of the sandwich, you're wondering? Me!

Part Two is my life story. You'll see how the choices I made throughout my life played out. My hope is that by sharing my personal experiences, ups and downs, enormous changes, and humorous stories, you will be able to see, hear, taste, smell, and feel what I know to be critical choices, making them more real for you. Ready to dive in? Let's get started!

"Tell me, what is it you plan to do with your one wild and precious life?"

—Mary Oliver, poet

PART ONE

Introduction to
The 5 Cornerstone Choices

What is the difference between a **choice** and a **decision**? "Decide" has word origins meaning "to kill off." A decision is the end of a selection procedure as it cuts or kills several options, while one of them is finalized. **Decision is the final result of a thought process that begins with choices or opportunities.**

Choice always precedes decisions. One reason this is so important to understand is that people, especially young adults, are bombarded with decisions. They are told by family, peers, teachers, guidance counselors, society, advertisers, and the media that they must decide on everything from their career to their shampoo. It starts to seem like every decision carries the same weight, that if you get your deodorant brand wrong, well…The relentless tidal wave of decisions often leads to extreme anxiety or depression—to relieve the pressure, poor decisions are made, especially about who to date and who to marry. (60% of all divorces happen during ages 25-39.)

We can surmise that decisions that feel forced upon us will probably not yield the results we would most like. Since choice always precedes decisions, it must be true that if you are making decisions left and right in order to avoid pressure, you have made the choice to live that way. You have surrendered your power. Instead of exercising your power to choose a life of fulfillment and freedom, you have chosen to consume a constant diet of other people's opinions.

When you are *deciding*, you engage the ego and are trying to figure out what is best for it (the ego). *What car will be most impressive to drive? What will make my dad happy? How can I get a job paying as well as my friend's?* External input is in the driver's seat. But when you *choose*, you surrender your will to something beyond yourself, trusting that it already knows what is best for you.

The Key is Yours to Claim

"Why isn't my life perfect yet?" This is how many young adults feel, as documented by psychologists studying what they term "the quarter-life crisis," akin to the common mid-life crisis, but applying to those in their late 20's and early 30's. More than ever before, young adults are suffering from anxiety or depression. No matter what your age, you can reclaim your power of choice and eliminate the stress of uncertainty that is so prevalent in today's world.

I know that pressure-packed decisions can make you want to just close your eyes and throw a dart, or do whatever your mom says, or become a bartender and avoid the whole responsible-adult scene. Whether you're struggling with career path issues, how to make new high-quality friends, dealing with conflicting needs to feel independent yet secure, this book will show you where to start.

To build your best life, start with foundational principles, cornerstone choices that support that goal. The key that we all hold is the power to choose.

Think of a time when you felt like you were the captain of your soul, the master of your fate. What I want you to know is that you can intentionally grow those seemingly random occasions into a solid place to stand, a powerful place from which to lead your life every day.

Choice not only precedes decisions, a choice made from your heart or gut will simplify your decision-making.

Reaching your full potential is a journey where your decisions and actions are informed by and consistent with your choices. In fact, there are only five primary ones to learn about and it is my privilege to share an overview of these now. In the next chapter, I'll discuss each one and show why it is essential to embrace for your life to be as full of joy as you can possibly imagine. When you embrace these cornerstone choices, you will find yourself able to authentically say that you never have a bad day.

The 5 Cornerstone Choices

1. **Choose to Love Yourself.** As a foundation, living with a clear sense that you love yourself allows for all other powerful gifts to be manifested in your life. This is not about living with disregard for

4

others—rather, it allows you to be more generous and supportive of others than you've ever been before.

2. **Choose to Be Yourself.** When you are true to yourself, you speak and act in ways that reflect who you are. You can access your self-expression and creativity. You won't exhaust yourself trying to please others.

3. **Choose to Own Your Own Power**. You have a unique perspective, talent, and genius. This doesn't mean that you have all the answers; it means you have all the resources you need, whether from your own strengths or from external sources you can tap into. When you know that you are an extraordinarily resourceful person, you will never see yourself as a victim.

4. **Choose to Help Others to Feel Alive and Connected.** Simply by being yourself and being constructive, you can profoundly impact others. When you are able to live this way, you will inspire others to do the same. This is the cosmic ripple effect: a single pebble breaking the water's surface has far-reaching effects. This choice brings vast and meaningful rewards that come from fulfilling our human need to contribute.

5. **Choose to Never Have a Bad Day**. When you live life oriented around these foundational choices, no matter what the obstacle or challenge life throws at you (and you'll have many, small and big), you can be in the driver's seat on the road of life. The stress of uncertainty will disappear. You'll find that you have a creative genius inside you that can surprise and amaze you on a regular basis. You will naturally attract other amazing people with similar values. You will live with such synergy that you fulfill one dream after another as you live into your fullest potential. You'll find that every single day gives you many things to feel grateful for.

You probably have some questions at this point. That would be natural. Here are some of the questions I've heard when I've presented The 5 Cornerstone Choices and, briefly, my answers:

Why does my mind create such a negative self-image? I'm always having to fight with my inner mean girl…it feels so hard to "choose to love myself" when I don't feel deserving at all.

YOU are not that mean girl. Keep heightening your awareness of the negative thought stream. Don't engage or "fight," just let everything float by.

Even though I KNOW what I should choose, sometimes I just can't make myself do it.

This is fear stopping you. When you are not present to life in the moment, you are struggling in the web of thoughts in your mind and that trap is a scary place! Become mindful of the task at hand, the experience of the present moment, and you will be free. Free to choose and act upon The 5 Cornerstone Choices.

How do I shift from feeling in a swirl of negative energy to being able to remember and make an empowering, positive choice?

This is a learnable skill. You can practice non-attachment. For sure, if you can relate to this question, you'll want to pay attention to Part Three of this book where you'll find resources and exercises to practice which will help and empower you. Now, you will have more questions answered in the next section, a guide which covers each choice more in-depth.

"You have been criticizing yourself for years, and it hasn't worked. Try approving of yourself and see what happens."

—Louise L. Hay

The 5 Cornerstone Choices

1 Choose to Love Yourself

Just as a home of lasting beauty and strength must be constructed on a well-built foundation, your achievements, joy, and meaningful experiences will grow to new heights with the strong and sturdy support of your commitment to yourself—choose to love yourself with the fierce determination that will withstand the harshest of external storms and influences.

This first choice is essential as a foundation for all other life choices. It's a journey, not a destination. It doesn't happen overnight. It's sometimes elusive, but always worth pursuing.

Who do you know right now that you're sure you will be around for the rest of your life?

There is only one person, for certain, that you will always live with—and whom you won't outlive. *You* are the one person that you'll always be with. So, it's important that you enjoy your own company, trust yourself, and recognize your good qualities.

Choosing to love yourself is not about living with disregard for others—rather, it allows you to be more generous and supportive of others than you've ever been before.

Every day, literally millions of people choose to take self-sabotaging actions that make it impossible to love themselves. They get a lot of free "help"—easy access, day and night. When you look out at the vast landscape of social media, do you not realize there are poisonous plants among the trees and flowers? Not everything is poisonous, but enough is there to kill your self-love and self-esteem.

This choice to love yourself can be difficult because of the constant exposure in social media of another's job, house, relationship status, body, vacation—comparing yourself to others steals your joy. Taking a break from social media can help to get rid of the overwhelming feeling of dissatisfaction with yourself. A recent study confirmed that: "Those who took a break from social media had significant improvements in well-being, depression and anxiety, compared with those who continued to use social media."

"If you're feeling like you use too much social media and this is negatively impacting your mental health, then taking a break may be worth a try and give you at least some short-term improvements," said study author Jeff Lambert, an assistant professor of health psychology at the University of Bath.

Beware of judges bearing gifts. "Here is a shiny new car to look at! Isn't it sleek and sexy? Imagine yourself driving this beauty! Because, after all, your car is old and boring by comparison. Your car says that you are boring, too. You'd be so much more attractive to sleek and sexy people if you also appeared sleek and sexy."

Who wants to hear such judgmental and shallow ranting? When you Choose to Love Yourself, you don't consume this poison.

Comparisons and external definitions of what is beautiful and what indicates success are not only a waste of time, they literally prevent you from living from the Choice to Love Yourself.

Focusing on how many "likes" or "followers" is the epitome of seeking external validation. When you learn to validate yourself, you won't be seeking external validation. Self-validation is the cornerstone of Choosing to Love Yourself.

Come up with your own measures of who you are and how you are doing—and how you are growing as a being. These are the only measuring sticks of lasting importance in your life.

When you don't feel full of love for yourself, you may try to get things from outside to fill you up: approval of others, time, money, status symbols. When you compare yourself, all that you had gained is lost as it leaks out. It is incredibly inefficient to keep using all your energy to fill up yourself from the outside-in, rather than from the inside-out. When you Choose to Love Yourself, it's an inside job.

"The more you like yourself, the less you are like anyone else, which makes you unique."

—Walt Disney

Hone each part of yourself to be accepted and appreciated by *you*. Then your inner strength will allow you so much freedom—you no longer will be compelled to seek external sources of fulfillment, over and over.

An extraordinary author and teacher, Shirzad Chamine, writes that each of us has an internal "judge" who attempts to rule (and ruin our day!). "The Judge's most damaging lie is that we are not worthy of love or respect by just being who we are. Instead, it forces us to constantly perform for them; this forms the construct of 'conditional love.' Most of us grow up experiencing love that is conditional on being good or performing, and we get into the habit of placing the same conditions on self-love. But conditional love is not real love. It's more like receiving a carrot for good behavior."—Shirzad Chamine, *Positive Intelligence*.

The people you surround yourself with are mirrors of how much you love yourself. Be mindful of the company you keep. Your friends are a reflection of the values you cherish. Are you around people who are of good character and who support you to be your best self? Are you around people who challenge you to view things with a different perspective, who are givers, who are ambitious? If not, re-examine your friend group. It is natural to become like the people you hang around most. If you have a lot of work to do in order to start both liking and loving yourself, add people to your inner circle who inspire you and motivate you to be a better version of yourself.

Re-train yourself about how you should be treated. Treating yourself with respect, compassion, and encouragement to be your best self are healthy and essential habits. (Not to mention, how can you expect others to treat you right if you don't treat yourself right?)

In **Part Three**, you will find a beautiful example about how to develop the habit of kind self-talk, written and contributed by my daughter, Ashley Soro, who is 31 at the time of this writing.

Think through your priorities. Don't answer the phone or reply to texts while you're busy with something important to you. Other people's needs can occupy several lifetimes' worth of our attention, and if you let them, they will.

While you can be available to others numerous times throughout the day, it is also important to carve out time for yourself that you can use to focus or recharge. If you constantly allow other people's phone calls, text messages, and social media alerts to distract you, you will delay your own progress and find yourself engulfed in other people's problems and issues. Put yourself first. You may be uncomfortable thinking of "love" as something to give to yourself. One helpful definition comes from scripture, 1 Corinthians 13:4-8 (New International Version):

> [4] Love is patient, love is kind. It does not envy, it does not boast, it is not proud. [5] It does not dishonor others, it is not self-seeking, it is not easily angered, it keeps no record of wrongs. [6] Love does not delight in evil but rejoices with the truth. [7] It always protects, always trusts, always hopes, always perseveres. [8] Love never fails…

Your relationship with yourself is the most important and longest relationship you'll ever have. It's worth spending the time and effort to develop a more loving relationship with yourself. Become aware of your negative self-talk and rewrite the script, giving your capable, unique self the green light in life to just go for it!

2 Choose to Be Yourself

The Self is the inner magic of who you are.

When you are true to yourself, you speak and act in ways that reflect who you are. You can access your self-expression and creativity. You won't exhaust yourself trying to please others.

Does this mean you should be insensitive or callous to others and justify your rudeness with, "Hey, this is just me…"? No, if you have a habit of being a jerk, then work on yourself until you have the habit of being awesome. Then, be yourself! (The person who is a jerk to others and the person who is afraid of social situations are, in actuality, not being themselves. Their real self is just being covered up with conditioned, fear-based thinking.)

> **"Waking up to who you are requires letting go of who you imagine yourself to be."**
>
> **—Alan Watts**

Our true self is who we really are when we let go of all of the stories, labels, and judgments that we have placed upon ourselves. It is who we naturally are without the masks and pretentiousness.

I've found that it is very much possible to just be yourself.

The countless stars in the sky are each a memorable moment in my life where a special outcome resulted from me just being myself. You'll read about many of these in the following chapters about my life.

Here's one that my daughter remembers to this day and urges me to tell the story that, to our family, is hilarious.

My wife, daughter, and I were seated at a Red Lobster restaurant and gave our server our dinner order. We sat with only our waters and waited, chatting and joking around as usual. When the three salads came, the server gave a napkin-rolled silverware set to my wife and daughter, but not to me. I was looking at the wonderful salad before me and did not notice until the server was gone. She did not return for several minutes, finally bringing the cheddar biscuits and asking if everything was okay.

Well, I'm what you'd call "spontaneous." Instead of politely asking her for a fork, I reached into my salad and pinched some lettuce, then with an exaggerated gesture, I brought the salad to my mouth while saying, "Oh, yes, everything is fine!" Before the server could leave again, I had used my fingers to grab salad three times right in front of her. You can't imagine how hard my wife and daughter were laughing, and yet the server never noticed why.

Now, the story concludes with me finally asking politely for silverware and the server profusely apologizing—at last understanding what had been so strange about our table of hilarity. When she promptly returned with my silverware, we got her to laughing, too.

It's the best feeling when you are just being yourself and those around you are entertained or uplifted. Your life will be more fulfilling as you share your natural self and you can't help but notice that others are inspired, influenced, and uplifted. When you are your natural self, others feel freer to be their natural selves. This is how you make a positive difference in others' lives. You can't authentically touch a person's life if you're wearing a cloak of pretense.

"To be yourself in a world that is constantly trying to change you is the greatest accomplishment."

—Ralph Waldo Emerson

Are you projecting a self or being yourself? Examples of projecting a self are anything you post on social media to show "this is who I am." No, it's not. That is only a story about you. You wrote it, you edited it, you published it. That is the "self" you choose to project.

Being yourself has absolutely nothing to do with others (whether or not they see your story).

"How can I tell if I'm being myself? Maybe my presentation is so ingrained I believe it's me. Sometimes I just draw a blank when I ask myself who I really am." This was shared with me by a 27-year-old, but I've heard the same sort of confusion from people in their 40's, 50's, and older!

If you don't put your hands firmly on the steering wheel, it doesn't matter how much time passes—you won't be connecting with what makes your life go *zoom!*

Be sure and do the exercises in Part Three, which are designed to be empowering. When you let go of the old ways of thinking, follow your bliss, and do what you love, you begin to align with happiness and peace. These are all indicators that you are connected with your true nature. You are then allowing your real self to shine forth in all its glory.

I know you'll recognize some of these self-talk examples which you can choose to ignore or change because it just doesn't serve you: "Once I perfect this or that, I can finally just be myself." Perfectionism is the idea or belief that if we look perfect, live perfect, and do everything perfectly, then we can minimize or avoid feelings of judgment, shame, or blame. It is a critical choice for you to let go of an inadequate feeling of "I am not enough" to take a triumphal stance of "I am enough." Believing you are enough is what gives you the courage to be authentic, vulnerable, and (naturally) imperfect.

"If only I were more like _____, I could be happy with myself." When you get started in a field you want to pursue, for example, it's completely valid to begin as an imitator of the most successful people in that field.

"I was a pretty good imitator of Roy Acuff, but then I found out they already had a Roy Acuff, so I started singin' like *myself*." —Hank Williams, award-winning singer/songwriter.

All through childhood, you were taught to think, speak, and behave like (fill in the blank). And it's very helpful to have a good role model you can imitate. (You will soon learn of my stories about how my dad was my role model.) But to truly come into your own and build your own life, you eventually need to embrace yourself as an original, a truly one-of-a-kind person! It's essential to find your OWN thing to build and bank on.

This is daunting to many people, because they feel it requires a miraculous act of creativity and uniqueness.

Not really, though. Eventually, imitation becomes influence. How you express yourself becomes a delicious stew of quality ingredients: inherited traits plus points of view, observations, experiences, interpretations, and styles you've picked up along the way.

"We are human beings, not human doings."

—Deepak Chopra

"To Do" can run our day from dawn to bedtime if we let it. We spend most of our time focusing on what we're doing, or would like to do, or have done, or haven't done. When we perceive that there is something wrong in our life, we ask ourselves, "What must I *do* to change this?"

"What's wrong with me? What did I do wrong? Why do I always make these mistakes?" **These questions require the mind to find reasons** to explain its discontents, and the mind is superb at providing reasons, justifications, and explanations.

If we look closely, we can see that whenever there is a sense of "have to," "must," "should," "ought," or "need to," we can suspect the presence of "To Do" in the driver's seat. Fortunately, we can learn to recognize and disengage from this mode.

Being: The Freedom Mode

"To Do" is not an enemy to be defeated, but learn to recognize when it is trapping you like a snare. The Being mode is a shift in perspective that helps you to step outside of your mind's tendency to overthink, over-analyze, and overjudge. So many young people today admit that they overthink everything!

In the To Do mode, the mind often travels forward to the future or back to the past, and the experience is one of not being "here" in the present much of the time.

In Being mode, the mind can focus fully on moment-by-moment experience, allowing us to be fully present and aware of whatever is here, right now. The Being mode involves a shift in our relation to thoughts and feelings. It is devoted to focusing on "accepting" and "allowing" what is, without any immediate pressure to change it, and no goal or standard to be reached.

In the Being mode, you can change your internal landscape, no matter what's happening around you. You are no longer dependent on external circumstances for your happiness, and you're back in control of your life. Not always easy, but very simple and always worthwhile.

Someone whose teachings have made a profound difference to me is Sadhguru, a mystic, author, and globally-renown person who serves humanity. In Part Three at the end of this book, I describe more about him and recommend his books—they are perfectly related to this topic of "Being."

How can you shift from feeling like a To Do machine into just Being?

This question points to the first and most important step: *catch yourself!* Stop and ask yourself, *What is my focus right now? Does that serve me?* If not, then state who and how you choose to be. In every moment you have an opportunity to ask yourself whether or not your way of being is empowering you.

The To Do focus will gradually deplete your inner resources and eventually leave you feeling drained, unfulfilled, and exhausted.

The Being level is where robust, sustainable change is created. Feeling the freedom to really live life is a sense of Being, never a To Do item to check off.

One way of stepping aside from the To Do mode and embracing the Being mode is to practice mindfulness meditation. This helps one to learn to *be with* whatever is going on and see the world as it is, not as one expects it to be, or what one fears it might become. You learn to allow thoughts and feelings to float, using the breath as an anchor to return to with gentleness and patience whenever the mind wanders off. Just notice what is happening without making judgments, seeing the experience as neither good nor bad. I have included an example for you in Part Three, your resources section.

With regular mindfulness exercises, you will start to understand that thoughts are just thoughts; they are events in the mind that are often valuable but they are NOT who you are.

Mindfulness brings you back, again and again, to full conscious awareness, a place of choice and intention. To be mindful means to be back in touch with one's senses, so one can see, hear, touch, smell, and taste things as if for the first time. I find this is invaluable to bring clarity to my thinking, especially when there seems to be a million things competing for my attention. I've learned that sorting out what is important and what is not gives me clarity and confidence to move forward easily.

Questions to find out whether you are locked in autopilot/doing mode:

- Do you find it difficult to stay focused on what's happening in the present?

- Do you tend to walk or drive quickly to get to where you're going without paying attention to what you experience along the way?

- Do you rush through activities without being really attentive to them?

- Do you get so focused on the goal you want to achieve that you lose touch with what you're doing right now?

- Do you find yourself preoccupied with the future or the past?

Be sure and try the mindfulness exercise found in Part Three.

3 Choose to Own Your Own Power

You have a unique perspective, talent, and genius. This doesn't mean that you have all the answers; it means you have all the resources you need, whether from your own strengths or from external sources you can tap into.

When you know that **you are an extraordinarily resourceful person**, you will never see yourself as a victim. Power comes from having an abundance of resources and the willingness to access them as needed.

Notice that this critical choice, as do the other four, puts your focus on you. Not the Instagram you. Not the best-selfie-pose you. Not the image of you that social media compels you to be consumed with and "working on." I am talking about who you are behind the mask. If your character, knowledge, and inner will had to make it all on their own…well, you can build, fortify, and nurture these to be an incredible source of power.

Fear of failure is the biggest reason many millennials are challenged with owning their power. As a young adult, you don't have much perspective. You don't realize how much time you have to make mistakes, get the lessons, grow and grow again.

Millennials today have lived through a recession which hurt college graduates looking for first career jobs. From a number of factors in today's society, many young people became pessimistic about their future and some have bought into the false story that they are victims. *Where does that get you?*

My friend's 8-year-old child intentionally fell on the playground in order to try and break her own arm. She had observed that a classmate who came to school with an arm cast was getting tons of attention—a line of kids even formed to have a turn signing her cast. The victim was getting much sympathy and what looked like popularity. But once the cast was off, all that aura disappeared. Imagine if she decided that the only way she could be noticed was to become injured again…maybe a foot cast next time! This is an example of childish logic, but some never seem to outgrow it! It is just as absurd for you to act like a powerless victim in order to "get" something. You don't win this way—you lose.

There is no rule or "should" that I can tell you about when the fruit of your adulthood is ready for you to pick and enjoy. Each person's timeline is somewhat different, naturally. What I want you to know is that no one knows except you. When you learn to tune into your inner voice and power, you can tell. You'll know if you are procrastinating about embracing your adult life's opportunities or if that is still on your horizon. When you have a sense that the time is right…CARPE DIEM! *Seize the day!*

But what does "owning my own power" look like?

True power is a quiet strength. It doesn't rely on adrenaline or a "rush" to provide a "feeling of power." It is also not based on the feeling of being in control. In my experience, the more controlling a person is trying to be, the less powerful they actually are. **True power is more accurately defined as knowing and using your strengths.** You can build on your strengths simply by having an intention to do so and being aware of your progress.

I find it's much better to identify, embrace, and build on your strengths rather than to focus on your weaknesses. An improved weakness is still not as good as a fortified strength, right?

You can use the exercise in Part Three to discover more about your strengths. Here are a few examples of what I mean by your "strengths." See if any of these describe you:

- Communication: It is natural for you to put your thoughts into words, whether spoken or written. You are a good conversationalist and enjoy sharing your ideas.

- Developing others: You see the potential in others…probably better than a person sees for himself. You get satisfaction from being a catalyst for others' personal or professional growth.

- Strong empathy: You feel more than sympathy or compassion, you feel what someone else is feeling. You can sense their feelings and imagine yourself in their situation.

- Enthusiasm: Others can feel your passion from a block away. Your positivity is contagious and you find that you effortlessly persuade others to become excited, too.

- Relationships: Connection is your middle name. You enjoy a variety of different types of people, finding a connection where others would not perceive one exists. Sometimes you are the essential glue holding a group together to work or play in a harmonious or constructive way.

4 Choose to Help Others to Feel Alive and Connected

Simply by being yourself and being constructive, you can profoundly impact others. When you are able to live this way, you will inspire others to do the same. This is the cosmic ripple effect: a single pebble breaking the water's surface has far-reaching effects—later deemed positive or negative.

I hope that you can hear the **opportunity** in Choosing to Help Others to Feel Alive and Connected, not a "should." The first step is to develop your own meaningful connections. Joy comes from feeling connected with yourself, with God, and with others. Depth of connection matters. Each meaningful connection that you make, nurture, and maintain has at least two beneficiaries. Your own intention and skill at connecting have a huge pay-off for yourself and for others.

Yet superficial connectedness appears to be quite tempting as technology threatens to supplant face-to-face intimacy. With devices in hand, one can avoid human exchange—and the potential awkwardness and risk therein.

Current research suggests that we do suffer without deep human connections. Someone recently told me a story: An older person was baffled by a teen's suicide since the deceased had over 300 Facebook friends. A younger person explained that Facebook friends are not necessarily real friends. You may have never met them, and they may not actually care if you live or die. Online friendship no longer connotes a precious relationship. We might think we are meeting our primal need via virtual solutions and high tallies of friends or followers, but it seems we are not.

According to MIT professor and researcher Sherry Turkle, author of *Reclaiming Conversation*, devices interfere with conversations, empathy, imagination, patience, resilience, inner life and mental health. Studies show that empathy is decreasing rapidly in rising generations.

As inner resources and empathy decline, depression, anxiety, and stress are soaring: College health services are inundated with students overwhelmed by depression, anxiety, stress, fragility, fear, loneliness, helplessness and a feeling of victimization.

What explains the suffering? The data indicates that young people are so stressed about grades, social media, and performance that they are sleep deprived, sheep-like and soulless. The very things that will help them succeed and stay well, such as meaningful relationships and conversations, are sacrificed. True connections take time to develop—and so many people are not giving them ample time.

Of course, starting in 2020, the Corona virus pandemic's austere isolation and anti-social practices didn't help. It did dramatically demonstrate that human connection is not only a preference but a requirement. People of all ages felt, to some degree, depressed, hopeless, or disconnected with their days void in depth and substance.

Another Benefit of Connecting

When you focus on authentic connection, any tendency to control others will fade away. We want to control others or situations because we're afraid of what might happen if we don't.

We connect in a way that can empower or influence people by being a model for others, not by forcing them to do things our way or to look at life our way.

> **"For to be free is not merely to cast off one's chains, but to live in a way that respects and enhances the freedom of others."**
>
> **—Nelson Mandela**

It is a deep human need to be a contribution—to someone, to some worthy cause, to your family—the opportunities are endless.

What if, simply by you fully enjoying your life, others around you began to more fully enjoy their own lives?

5 Choose to Never Have a Bad Day

When you live your life out of these foundational choices, no matter what the obstacle or challenge life throws at you (and you'll have many, small and big), you can be in the driver's seat on the road of life. The stress of uncertainty will disappear.

You'll find that you have a creative genius inside you that will surprise and amaze you on a regular basis. You will naturally attract other amazing people with similar values. You will live with such synergy that you fulfil one dream after another as you live into your fullest potential. Every single day will provide you with many things to feel grateful for.

"But what if others prevent me from not having a bad day?" We have all been in numerous situations, either at work or at home, that have been irritating or frustrating. Perhaps one of your co-workers is being unreasonable, one of your friends won't stop complaining about their significant other, or you discover that a family member you loaned your car to returned it with a dent and an empty gas tank. Rather than letting these situations upset or infuriate you, train yourself to use them as an opportunity to learn something worthwhile and to grow.

Remember, no matter how much you shoot arrows at life's challenges, they'll never stop showing up. You can't dodge them, either. So, the only thing that makes sense is to accept this fact and choose how you'll respond—i.e., how to get something akin to lemonade out of lemons.

Is "never having a bad day" just wishful thinking? When you decide it's time to start living your life as someone who "never has a bad day," it can, indeed, be so. At one point in time, traveling to the moon was only wishful thinking. A person born into a poor family becoming extremely wealthy was only wishful thinking. Never having a bad day does not have to just be wishful thinking. When the time is right (and that is up to you), it can be so, I promise you.

In Part Two, I'll cover many stories from my own life which will show you that no matter where you came from or what cards you've been dealt, you can Choose to Never Have a Bad Day. Yes, even you!

Once I was asked if there is a "science of happiness." In fact, there is. When you understand how the brain functions to release chemicals that significantly affect your mood, you can start to see why it is truly within your power to "never have a bad day." The fact is that you can intentionally activate these mood-uplifting chemicals found in your own physiology. Isn't that great news?

**Your own chemistry is the essential catalyst
for your choice to never have a bad day.**

Generally, *dopamine* is associated with pleasure and reward behavior. *Serotonins* act as a mood stabilizer and help to prevent depression. *Endorphins* can elevate your mood and block pain. *Oxytocins* provide feelings of love and trust.

It's common to be more aware of negative feelings, but then you can adjust the chemical balance in your brain to cultivate and sustain positive emotions. It's actually simple: positive thinking (which just means being aware of your thoughts and choosing which ones to focus on), mindfulness exercises, practicing gratitude, and physical exercise are your means to the end (of never having a bad day).

In Part Three, you'll find a great collection of ideas for daily ways to feed yourself the best diet of positivity Also, my daughter Ashley, a nationally-recognized fitness professional, contributed her insights and best tips in "Choosing to Love Yourself Starts with Good Health and Self-Compassion."

When you think about it, it should be no surprise that the natural and organic science of our bodies supports us to have a purposeful and joyful life—if we take the appropriate actions. There is nothing in your basic design which prevents you from never having a bad day. It's a *choice*.

Do you believe it's possible to never have a bad day? What you end up accomplishing and enjoying in your life depends a great deal on what you believe is possible. What you believe is possible depends on **what you tell yourself** and what you think about yourself each day. If you want to change your reality, change your thoughts and beliefs. For me, that means saying positive words of affirmation each morning. It means reading devotionals and inspirational stories that help open my mind to what is possible. I tell myself that I will approach every situation as an opportunity to grow, so I can view situations more positively. I tell myself that I am loved so I never doubt my self-worth. What things do you tell yourself? What beliefs do you have? What thoughts do you think? Your answers will shape your reality.

In *Have a Great Day*, one of the many best-selling books on positive thinking by the late Rev. Norman Vincent Peale, he shares this anecdote: "In a twisting little street in Kowloon [Hong Kong], I passed a shop where tattooing was done. Pictured in the window were some suggestions: a mermaid, a flag, and the motto 'Born to lose.' I was so astonished by the latter that I entered the shop and asked the man if anyone had ever had those words actually tattooed into their skin. 'Yes, a few,' he said. But then, in his broken English, he added a wise insight: 'Before tattoo on body, tattoo on mind.'"

My reality is that I've never had a bad day. How can this be? You'll see how I have lived for more than six decades when you learn about my story in the following chapters: born into a family of modest means who lived in a minority community in Iraq; accompanied my mother who fled the country; ended up in America where I soon came to believe that anything was possible. My successes thus far include the most beautiful and loving family anyone could hope for, memory-making adventures in many different US cities, and entrepreneurial accomplishments and wealth beyond my wildest dreams.

While I will share with you my very best attempt to describe how I can honestly say I've never had a bad day, the "how to" is not as useful to you as The 5 Cornerstone Choices I have distinguished and distilled for you to take on as your own. Nevertheless, here is how I live each day:

My day is my air that I breathe. I let go of emotions that don't serve me well. My day is my air that I breathe, so I let go of things I cannot control; I create simplicity in my life and enjoy every moment of the day.

My day and I are worthy of love and kindness; I choose self-compassion because it's about my day.

I acknowledge and embrace my uniqueness. I treat myself and my day with respect. I love and approve of myself and am kind to myself; my day and I are both worthy, I feel good about the day and myself. I accept myself just the way I am as my day acknowledges my strengths and weaknesses and I keep floating,

I honor my day and the best part of myself. I realize that making mistakes is human. I forgive myself for my past mistakes as I learned from each one.

I honor my life's journey every day, I value and acknowledge my hard work and effort, I thank my day and recognize my progress no matter how small. I appreciate the day, and I believe in my achievements with grace. I am proud of myself.

I am focused on the positive aspects of myself. I have a positive self-image. I have empowering self-talk. I put my trust in my inner guidance and I have a rational way of looking at situations. I set realistic expectations for myself; it's easy for me to cope with imperfections.

I am free of self-criticism, my inner dialogue is constructive. I am resilient. I focus on the value of my work.

I boldly act on the opportunities that are good for me. I am confident of my abilities to succeed and I accept and appreciate the compliments I receive. I acknowledge my success, I celebrate my success, and I am my own cheerleader.

I am at peace with my failures. I handle the feedback on my work with grace and openness as I have an open mind. I am willing to try out new things for my progress. I am free of attachments to the result.

I love and honor myself no matter what. I am thankful for my life and I understand that what I say to myself can make or break my life. My perception about myself is essential. Through inner guidance, I let go of the inner critic that questions my abilities.

I believe and manifest for the highest good of all concerned, including myself.

This is how I live…how I've always lived since I was a child. My story defies logic and is unexplainable in common terms. This book isn't as much about me as it is about how my unusual life story can shed light on your own experiences, questions, and desire to develop yourself and create a life that you love.

What I Most Want for You

I have lived my life knowing that nature loves courage. Therefore, I would love for my readers to have the courage to step out and away from limiting beliefs. Build your life using The 5 Cornerstone Choices. Remember that "possibility" is always found within "impossibility," yes?

Every amazing discovery in history was the result of someone being bold. Being bold is intrinsic to orienting around The 5 Cornerstone Choices. These are intertwined and synergistic, in that the 5 Choices support being bold, while being bold enables you to embrace The 5 Choices and have the extraordinary experience of living life fully.

As you read my story, I want you to feel validated in your hope that the world is not here to grind you down, but to lift you up. This is how magic is done.

We come with nothing, we go with nothing, but one great thing we can achieve in our beautiful life is a little remembrance in someone's mind and a small place in someone's heart.

I don't know the author but these words are ones I find memorable: "Look back and get experience. Look forward and see hope. Look around and find reality. Look within and find yourself."

This book is for anyone ready to look within themselves and also be open to accept guidance for charting a happy and deeply satisfying course for life. You don't have to go it alone. You don't even have to do anything, ever. It's your choice…but I will emphasize that there's no time like the present!

Let's begin Part Two—*wow, do I have some stories for you!*

"We cannot put off living until we are ready. The most salient characteristic of life is its coerciveness: it is always urgent, 'here and now' without any possible postponement. Life is fired at us point blank."

—Jose Ortega y Gasset

PART TWO

"There are only two lasting bequests we can hope to give our children. One of these is roots, the other, wings."

—Johann Wolfgang von Goethe

CHAPTER ONE

Paradise

My father was born in Iraq, in "Aradin," which means a place of fertile lands, clean air, clear water, and clement weather—paradise.

This area has history that for most people is unfathomable. There is still a church there which was built over one thousand years ago, for example.

The Sultana Mahdokht Church in Aradin, dating from the 4th century, named to commemorate Sultana, the patron saint of Aradin (executed for her religious beliefs in the year 319). Today, it is a pilgrimage site for many Chaldean Catholics and other Christians.

Babylonian King Nebuchadnezzer II (who ruled between 605 and 562 BC), according to legend, built the famous Hanging Gardens of Babylon (one of the "Seven Wonders of the Ancient World") near Aradin. Depicted in artworks, the gardens included date palms, blossoming flowers, and imported plants including willow, cypress, and ebony. Incredibly, currently secured at Yale University, you will find a recipe collection originating from this area in the seventeenth century B.C. These are believed to be the oldest known recipes anywhere in the world and the first documented cookbooks in human history.

The village of Aradin is located in the north of Iraq about 95 miles from the large city of Mosul. Approximately 250 miles north of Baghdad and 110 miles southeast of the city of Cizre in Turkey, Mosul stands on the west bank of the Tigris River, opposite the ancient Assyrian city of Nineveh on the east bank. Nineveh is one of the oldest and greatest cities in antiquity and was settled as early as 6000 BC. In the prominent Sebna Valley, Aradin sits between the mountains of Metina at the north and Kara on the south.

I have stood in Nineveh looking up at the mountains. Even without knowing their history, they occurred to me as ancient and permanent masters of the terrain, not in the least bit shaped or affected by mankind. I imagined that every large outcropping of stone had a story to tell. And each story spans thousands of years.

Long after the mountains made their first impression on me, I learned that they do actually hold ancient stories, immortalized as sculptured rock reliefs. The rock reliefs of Iraqi Kurdistan span several centuries, beginning with the mid-third millennium BC, as noted by New York's Columbia University field archeologists (https://mcid.mcah.columbia.edu/art-atlas/mapping-mesopotamian-monuments/rock-reliefs).

Knowing that I am the son of people with bloodlines tracing back to the beginning of civilization affects me in ways I can't explain. I have no desire to dwell today in this part of world, but I am grateful for the unique perspective I have inherited on culture, longevity, and the importance of food preparation and family.

My mother, also from the northern part of Iraq, was born in Baqofa, about 15 miles north of Mosul. The earliest historical reference to her village dates to the 7th century. In my mother's time, the inhabitants adhered to the Chaldean Catholic Church and spoke the Syriac language. Dominican friars first came to the area in the thirteenth century. The inhabitants of Aradin were converted to Chaldean Catholicism in the 1830s by Joseph Audo, archbishop of Amadiya and Dominican missionaries.

So my mother, Siham Daoud, and father, Yousif Toma Soro, both grew up in the north of Iraq. Dad attended school until fifth grade, but Mom did not have even that opportunity. Dad's side of the family owned considerable land for farming vegetables, fruits, and walnuts. Concentrating on farming during the summer months, they had to produce an abundance of food to last through the winter and used underground cellars as their means of refrigeration and preservation.

Because of constant wars in northern Iraq between the Iraqi government and Kurds, most people left and moved to the largest city in Iraq—Baghdad, the cradle of civilization. This was where my mom and dad first met.

While attending his cousin's wedding, my dad noticed a nearby apartment building with families coming and going. One young woman caught his attention as she walked along with another woman, smiling and talking in a light-hearted conversation. Something about her captured his interest and he decided to find out who she was. His cousin told him that he knew that the girl lived there with her family and that she was not quite 15 years old. But most importantly, he knew that she had a protective and vicious older brother and any approach could be dangerous.

We know the eventual outcome, but there's no telling how much courage my dad had to muster to go over to where the young woman lived and ask to speak with her parents. They were receptive to talk with him and then agreed upon an arrangement when he asked for her hand in marriage.

And so, Mom, 14, and Dad, 24, were married. In a town area called Al Murabaha in Al Rasheed Street, they found one bedroom to lease. Their first home together, then, was within a large house where many different families were living, which was a common arrangement at that time. Dad walked over a mile to work every day. He worked as a server at a mansion-sized house for a high-ranking politician from England, and that's where he learned how to speak English.

As I learned more history, I thought it was ironic that a British gentleman living near Al Murabaha helped my father learn English; earlier, the British were defeated and chased out of the area by the Ottomans, who ruled Iraq from 1534 to 1918.

My Happy Childhood Begins

Dad proved himself to be invaluable to his boss and they became very close. A few years went by, and Dad's dependents had grown to include my oldest sister, my brother, and me.

Fortunately, his boss was kind enough to offer our family the guest house on the mansion's property. We were able to live there until the diplomat was transferred out of Iraq to return to England, less than one year after we moved in.

Then my cousin rented to us one available room he had. Dad soon got another job as a waiter at the Sheraton Hotel. After a few months, thanks to his good English, he was promoted to dining room manager. Then we were able to move to a town called Garage Amana.

Our Garage Amana house had six bedrooms. A luxurious space for our family to enjoy? Of course not. We contracted to lease the entire house and then immediately my mother started renting the extra five bedrooms. Our family lived there with another five families, all of us in the same house with only one bathroom. Every morning when everyone was starting their day and many were getting ready to go to work or school, we waited in line for a turn in the bathroom. It was a typical inconvenience, not something people complained about.

Each family lived in their one room. At that time, my older brother Basim was living with our grandmother in Aradin, so it was Mom, Dad, my older sister Basima, and me. There was always a hustle-bustle as you would imagine, yet every day's creative purpose seemed to be to generate a good time for all. Our family found entertainment in dancing, socializing at the parks, going to friends' houses, and sleepovers for the children. (Perhaps the adults had an understanding that accepting visiting children from other families ensured a future favor returned, thus offering a brief respite and privacy.) Of course, boys played soccer and girls helped mothers with cleaning, cooking, and laundry—all by hand, no washer or dryer.

Soon my brother and our grandmother came from Aradin to join the family. Being together was more important than any consideration of our limited indoor space. But outside was a whole wide world. The sandy clay street we were living on was nearly 400 yards long, yet so narrow that only one car could pass. From the beginning to the end of the street, all the houses were attached and painted in different colors. My sister, brother, and I waited each morning for a school bus to pick us up to go to the Catholic school. In the afternoon, the bus dropped us off at the street and then we had to walk about 200 yards to get to our house.

There was never a minute to be lonely or bored. One of my happy memories is from playing in the street along with my brother. Sometimes, I would watch as my brother swallowed his gulp of a Pepsi–Cola, eager for him to pass the glass bottle to me for my victory swig, taking my turn as did each of our teammates. Everyone enjoyed a refreshing sip of the soda, which we rarely had except after earning a share of the prize drink when we won a game.

The game was soccer, with our long, narrow street as the field. The ball—never what you might picture as a stitched, black-and-white leather soccer ball—was different every time. Our roundish ball was made from scraps we found on the street or from home: cloth, small pieces of tire rubber, wads of paper. I think the author of the adage "where there's a will, there's a way" had observed our creative handiwork and patch jobs to make our ball last a whole game.

It was pure fun racing up and down our street, knowing that behind each doorway were our own families, no doubt cooking some delicious foods for us to devour later in the evening. The Pepsi-Cola was not really why we played so hard, but it was a symbolic celebration.

I wasn't a big fan of school. I didn't care about history because that had already passed; spelling and writing were just too tedious; I didn't care about geography because I knew I could not travel; the only thing I really liked was to play sports. I played basketball, soccer, volleyball, track and field. Yes, I did get in a lot of mischief and often my dad was asked to come and talk to the principal to solve the problem. As I was failing the sixth grade, Mom had a plan for me to go and live with my grandparents, a half-hour away. Not my idea of a good plan! The only thing to do at their house was to be quiet and study. I had no choice but to go there and focus on my school work for a change. My grades improved a lot and I graduated from primary school.

My First Blonde and My First Job

My most vivid memory from that time in my life comes from an American movie, a Western. I was sitting in front of the television, next to my dad, and with the rest of the family, we watched *The Misfits* with Clark Gable and Marilyn Monroe.

I was completely taken with the beautiful, blonde Marilyn Monroe. I had never seen a woman anything like her before. I fell in love. I told Dad, "One day when I am old enough, I will marry my bride just like Marilyn Monroe."

Dad laughed. He responded that there weren't any blondes anywhere around, but he wished me the best of luck.

When I returned from my grandparents' back home, I learned that my father had left. My mother anxiously told me that he'd had to flee from powerful people with opposing politics and hide in northern Iraq. Dad belonged to the Kurdistan Democratic party and the Iraqi government wanted to kill him. Fortunately, my uncle worked under Saddam Hussein and heard of plans to have my father hanged. He had immediately come to our house and helped my father escape.

For about six months, my dad was nowhere to be found. I had a gut feeling that he was safe and that my attention needed to be on helping my mother. I told her I wanted to help support her and the family. Mom was forced to go to work and she found a job at the Carlton Hotel. Her pay was three dinars for the whole month, which was the equivalent of nine dollars. At that time, she accepted it because it was better than nothing. With my dad gone, our family was greatly impacted and we experienced what it's like when something as basic as food is scarce. For our school lunch, we carried Arabic bread rolled up with fried potatoes and lots of rice, lentils, or cracked whole wheat, but rarely with any meat.

Realizing how dire our family's situation was and that three dinars was simply not sufficient, I begged my mother to let me go to work with her. I figured that at my age of nearly 15 and my willingness to work hard, the hotel would find something for me to do. Mom reluctantly had to agree that this was necessary and allowed me to work for the hotel as a door boy.

I was pleased to earn two dinars a month to help the family and to proudly wear the door boy uniform. I stood by the front entrance of the hotel for 12 hours a day, opening and closing the door, saying *good morning, good afternoon, good evening, good-bye.* Now Mom and I were earning five dinars a month, around 15 dollars, which was better than nothing.

Open. Close. All day. The hotel was busy, but I soon became bored. The entrance doors were very tall and made of heavy glass. I did enjoy greeting each patron and seeing who seemed to take any notice. But, because I could see through the glass who was approaching and who was leaving, my boredom was growing. I started looking at the cars that would come to the hotel and found this an interesting diversion. All were covered in dust. Some were very dirty, coming in from all over the Middle East—Saudi Arabia, Kuwait, Syria, Lebanon, and other Iraqi cities.

After work one day as my mother and I walked home (a good three miles each way), I told her about an idea I had and persuaded her to talk to the hotel general manager the next day. She was successful in convincing him to invest in supplies and tools required for washing cars. He agreed to my plan of washing cars as a courtesy service to hotel guests. No one asked the guest or told them about this, we just let them walk out of the hotel and find their car sparkling clean. They would walk back into the hotel and ask the receptionist how their car got cleaned and she would say "the door boy." So I solved my boredom issue, started making good tips every day, and made the general manager happy, too.

Next, I added yet another courtesy service for guests. I would ask them if they wanted a shoeshine, and the majority of them said yes! My earnings were amazing—two or three dinars every day! It felt great to have money in my pocket, but even better to support my family, including my grandmother. My mother was astounded at how much money I gave her to buy our food. Instead of only once a week, we were able to have meat every day. I felt like a millionaire! My mother was very good about saving money, too, and my enterprises were helping us save for our future, whatever that would bring.

Doing my three jobs at the hotel became more and more challenging as my services grew in popularity. People would bring their luxury cars to me to wash even if they were not staying at the hotel. The general manager soon realized that I was making more money that he was. A lot more! His solution was to fire me and take over the car wash business himself. He did not even want to keep working as the manager because he saw where the opportunity was. He made a contract with the hotel, which set up a new building space for him to wash the cars.

Mom's New Job and Important Connections

Mom stayed working at the hotel while my father was away, still hiding in northern Iraq. I can only imagine how challenging this time was for my mom, having to work so hard to support herself and her children, all the while worried sick about my dad. She was determined to find a better job, at least one to ease the financial burdens.

One of the hotel employees working in the office was sympathetic toward her, knowing she wasn't making sufficient money at the hotel. One day she told her that she knew of a possible opportunity for her to make a lot more money. Mom was skeptical at first, but said she wanted to know more. The office clerk told her that a large newspaper company was looking for a contractor to clean their eight-story building, seven days a week. Mom instantly knew she could gather other workers and become that "contractor" and she followed up on the lead. She was hired! With 20 women helping her, Mom took on the challenge and started making more money than she had imagined was possible in her situation. Early every morning, the company bus came to our neighborhood, picked up the crew of women, and took them to the building.

I believe that was the only newspaper which was allowed in the country and the majority of the content was about (supporting) the Iraqi government. The president of the news agency was Tariq Aziz, who later became Iraq's Vice President and Saddam Hussein's right-hand man!

As is the habit of many top executives, Aziz was usually the first one to arrive to work each morning. Often, only the cleaning crew was there and that is how it happened that Mom got to know Tariq Aziz. One day, in a friendly conversation, he asked Mom about her husband and she told him the story. He made a few calls and my father was found and safely returned to us!

I remember being very happy to have my dad back home. I remember that my mother too was very happy, but also that she didn't act like she was relieved that he had finally come to our rescue—she had become a resilient and enterprising person who stepped up to meet the responsibility of taking good care of herself and her children. This strength would be tested by even more difficult challenges soon enough.

On the Shores of the Tigris River

The news agency building was on the most popular street in Baghdad, in the midst of much of the city's activity. The street's route was quite ancient, located on the eastern bank of the Tigris River and ran with it, extending between the Republic Bridge (Queen Alia Bridge) in the eastern Bab area and the suspension bridge in the eastern Karrada region. This street was named after the poet Abu Nuwas, who died in Baghdad in the year 199 AH (814 AD).

Tigris River, Baghdad, Iraq (c. 1972)

Throughout the history of Baghdad and especially in the last century, this was one of the most important areas of the evening and the "Samar," which essentially means socializing at night with conversation, poetry, and music. Similar to a modern "river walk," many shops and cafes faced the street as it extended along the shore of the Tigris River. The cafes each pulsed with life in the bustling area, contrasting between the simple and the high-end, yet all with a commonality: to prepare and serve the traditional dinner of *Masgouf,* grilled fish. For thousands of years and even today, this is considered the national dish of Iraq. Today, if I could obtain fresh carp from the Euphrates River (the same one mentioned in the Bible's

Garden of Eden!), I would gather fresh herbs and tomatoes and prepare this flavorful dish all the time (served with vermicelli rice, of course!).

With the cafes' aromas wafting onto the sidewalks, patrons entered to enjoy other traditional and delicious meals such as *tikka*, *kebab*, and *baja* with *sinkin* (heavy, dark, Iraqi tea). All of that was accompanied by the sounds of the songs of the Lady of the East, Umm Kulthum, the most popular performer in all of Iraq. Umm Kulthum recorded 300 songs over a 60-year career and her words of love, loss, and longing still drift from taxis, radios, and cafes, 45 years after her death.

In the West, her influence on popular music surpasses her fame among the general public. But those who knew, knew; she's been acknowledged by Led Zeppelin, Bob Dylan, and U2, among other musicians who discovered her mesmerizing music, most of it comprised of complex Arabic poetry.

Of course, Tariq Aziz was a member of the most exclusive dining club on Abu Nuwas Street. Many top government officials frequented this club, which was even named after the Minister of Information. At that time, the club was having a lot of issues with the person who was running the establishment. There was no room for tolerating problems when the most privileged high-ups in the country expected the club to be excellent in every way.

Aziz was involved in the urgent task of turning the club around. From my mother, he knew that my father had been in the hotel business, so Aziz asked my mother if her husband would be interested in taking over the club. Dad was very excited to have this opportunity and he gladly took on the challenge.

The Garden of Eden and Two Very Different Brothers

The restaurant was large, luxurious, and lush with natural beauty. The patio adjunct to the dining room was a garden of roses, other flowers, and palm trees. A true oasis in the middle of the city. Seating easily accommodated 250-300 member diners, but retained the intimacy with each setting. Every detail was elegant, with every server wearing a tuxedo. My dad soon had the place running like a clock, an excellent staff, formal-style service, and chefs preparing superb Middle Eastern cuisine.

Only members and their guests were allowed in the club. My brother and I helped Dad with his large responsibility of running the business. I worked at almost every position in the club, quickly learning to bus tables, become a server, and even a bartender with Dad alongside, behind the bar. My brother didn't care for any role and was constantly at odds with Dad, but I fell in love with the business.

I realized that I'm a people person and the club environment suited me well. We operated from six in the evening until two in the morning. During the day, we received from vendors all of our beverages, supplies, and food. Every day, one of us had to be there to receive beverages at 7 a.m., and then the dry and perishable items between 9 a.m. and 3 p.m. Since it was necessary for Dad to sleep during the day, either my brother or I were tasked with receiving product. We could leave at 5 p.m. when Dad came in—my brother was quick to take off but I would always stay. I loved the business, plus I loved making serious money for the first time in my life.

Things did not improve between Dad and my brother. They were always fighting and my brother felt he could not continue that way. He convinced our mother that he really needed to make a big change in his life. He wanted her to persuade Dad to allow him to leave Iraq! His plan was to go to Lebanon and ask the United States for asylum. His goal was to go to America as a refugee. One factor that probably helped to get Mother's approval was that if he left Iraq, he could avoid being conscripted for military service. That can be a nightmare, with you never knowing how long the term required, some men forced to stay serving 25-30 years! So, Mom and Dad agreed; my brother got his wish and left for Lebanon.

At 15, I was safe from the draft and was supposed to be attending middle school. I went for about a month, hating every minute. My head and heart were always elsewhere, namely the club. Lucky for me, it was clear that Dad could not run the business by himself, so I decided to quit school to work full-time. Under the circumstances, my parents were okay with it. For me, I was on top of the world! I was extremely happy being where I felt I belonged—that is, at the club day and night, seven days a week. The members got to know and admire me for my obvious enthusiasm for every aspect of my work. I was floating on air, chatting with customers, and being of service.

Wins for Everybody!

One of the member Directors asked my dad if we could start bringing in some kind of entertainment at the club. Dad told him he would look into it and see what he could do. When I heard about entertainment being needed, I got hold of my friends and I asked each one what instrument they liked to play. My idea was to gather my friends, form a band, and fill the bill as the club's live entertainment.

Now, remember that my family and friends were living in an impoverished area, and it was only recently that my family and I had started to do well financially. If I wanted a band, I would need to fund it, which I was thrilled to do! From the tips I had earned, I bought everyone's instruments—a keyboard, drum set, guitar, and a bass guitar for myself. There was never a thought about spending my money on these things; my heart was expanding as I helped others, and I could see this helped me in return. I was the only one who could not play very well, but I made it up with singing!

But what did we sing? Popular Western music was what we imagined big-city club bands played, so that's what we performed, as well as Arabic and Assyrian Chaldean music. Our debut was in front of 250 people and yet I was not nervous at all. I was ready to sing the handful of English-sounding words I had memorized. We played a Tom Jones hit with the lyrics "sheeza-lay-dee...whoa, whoa, whoa, sheeza-lay-dee." Repeat. And again. Then we played a Santana song, "Black Magic Woman," and those were the only three words sung, repeated for about five minutes until we decided to end the song and move on to Elvis or Chubby Checker. Luckily our band could play the tunes very well and our audience was probably as clueless as we were about what any of the words even meant!

And having my father experiencing all this was more than a treasure to me. I remember seeing him standing to the side of the area he had quickly transformed into a dance floor. He was in tears from enjoying watching me having so much fun and receiving all this attention from the members for what we had accomplished. A dream come true, by knowing everything impossible could be turned around to possible! From the start of the event until the end, people were dancing and having so much fun. That night and all the days following, the members were thanking my father for providing the entertainment, arranged so quickly. Back in those days, there was not much family entertainment besides waiting for a celebration like a wedding. The club was sold out every Thursday and Friday night!

My friends to this day thank me for what I did for them. Everyone in the band embraced the idea and later went on to become career musicians—and in fact became very successful and well-known in Iraq. This experience was instrumental in my discovery that the Choice to Help Others to Feel Alive and Connected is a key cornerstone choice.

A Tragic "Lesson"

It was 1974, and I was 17 years old. The loudest voice I had ever heard in my life woke me up. It was my dear mother's scream of horror and despair when she saw my father, completely unconscious, being carried into our home by my cousin and a taxi driver.

Dad and my cousin had been getting ready to close the restaurant when five men showed up at the front door. The tallest of the five, apparently the leader, looked down at my father. "We're looking for Yousif. Do you know him?" he asked.

My father looked the tall man in the eyes and answered, "I am Yousif." Three of the men stepped in and began shooting questions at my dad. Even as they approached closer and closer to him, he refused to answer anything. He certainly wasn't going to tell them about the anti-government meetings he had been organizing right there at that restaurant.

They kept pressing him and came right out and threatened to hurt him. My father was no stranger to fighting, but only when fueled by alcohol. The three men surrounded him and suddenly his rage sent him into a full-out brawl—one against three. He managed to control the fight and ran outside to confront the other two, telling them all to leave. Soon he found himself in a fist-fight against five men. One came up behind him and clubbed him over the head with a gun.

He lost consciousness and fell backwards, his head hitting the concrete with a noise so loud my cousin heard it and came running out. The men matter-of-factly told my cousin exactly what had taken place. They wanted him to know that this was to teach my father a lesson not to mess with the government, and then they drove away.

Dad was very sympathetic to the Kurds. He was born and raised in Kurdistan, and his only brother (Shleamoun) was killed in the war at the age of 26. Dad did not become a soldier for the fight, but often met with the Kurdish leader and did anything he could to help Kurds. The Iraqi government launched a campaign of forced deportation and exile targeting the Feyli Kurds due to their ethnic background and Shia religion.

Dad was a member of the Kurdistan Democratic Party and the Iraqi government found out from an informant that my father was holding meetings at the club during the day when the establishment was closed.

Saddam Hussein was not then officially Iraq's ruler, but he ran everything. He had sent his men "to teach the man a lesson."

My father and, in fact, our whole family never recovered from that cruel lesson that was unfortunately typical in that tyrannical dictatorship. My mother's scream had awakened not only me but dozens of people. As my father lay on the floor with blood draining from his nose, mouth, and ears, all of us saw the writing on the wall; he was dying. When a few of our closest relatives arrived, they helped my mother get him transported to the hospital.

We all waited anxiously at the hospital until finally a doctor told them the prognosis. My father had incurred severe brain damage and would live two or three days, but was not expected to regain consciousness. Right then and there I witnessed my mother's heart split into tiny pieces. She would not even have a chance to say goodbye.

After two days, my father passed away. I never want back to the club. Mom refused to go back to work. Life as we had known it was over and we were for the first time in our lives in a state of shock.

Finding strength when your foundation seems to crumble under you— that is not always easy, but it is always a choice you can make.

I am a Product of Unconditional Love

I was very close to both Mom and Dad. I liked to observe my dad as I wanted to understand his way of thinking, his feelings, and perceptions. I decided he was the wisest, most intelligent man I knew. I not only admired him, I wanted to learn how to be like him; especially I wanted to be as intuitive. His death left me with an emptiness; simultaneously, with a heart more full of compassion and clarity around what is truly important in life.

With my mom, I had always felt a strong heart connection. I admired her for how she could be both strong and soft. After my dad had been killed and was no longer our family's leader and protector, I devoted myself to assuring her that there was nothing to worry about. I let her know that I would always be there for her, and would never let her down.

From that time on, I never lived a lifestyle of being alone. I gladly welcomed the role of taking care of my family, especially my mom, because it never,

ever felt like a burden to me. When you understand that life is about service, you only see opportunities to serve.

My mom was brave, strong, and full of love for us. She could not read nor write and she never went to school. Yet, she was able to make an extremely hard decision very quickly: we must leave Iraq. Her decision would change the course of our family's history. Her wise decision to move to another country was so fast that people envy her to this day.

When I was a child, my mom and dad gave me the greatest gift of all—the gift of unconditional love. They cared deeply about who I would become and much less about what I would do. Compassion is at the heart of every little thing I do and the dearest quality I possess. If I ever lose compassion, I would stop being human. My mother protected me from the world, and my father confronted me with it. My spark came from this love. I knew it and I planned to make my life reflect love for my own seed of goodness within and for others. At that point in my life, it was my honor to protect my mother until we all felt safe again.

I am grateful for the years I had with my dad, my greatest teacher, and it's a shame the time was abruptly cut short. Thankfully he imparted to me a burning desire for not just experience, but wisdom. Ever since I can remember, I have been interested in what wise people had within them, and what they said that I could learn from. Though I don't know who to attribute many things to, I was like a sponge for what I could pick up that had a clarion ring of truth to it.

"Happiness is the new rich." "Constant kindness can accomplish much." "Kindness is caring for others, even when they may not care for you." "Love and kindness are never wasted."

My mom and dad were never able to provide our family with our own house, much less a grand house, but my memories from childhood are ones of abundance. Words cannot convey how full of life and love my memories are. Nothing from the outside world took dominance over the heart and soul of our family. I learned at a very early age that love is a force more formidable than any other. It is invisible—it cannot be seen or measured, yet it is powerful enough to transform you in a moment and offer you more joy than any material possession could. When I was not yet four years old, this invisible force enveloped me one day, a kind of awakening occurred, and my fate was set.

My Enlightenment

An enlightened human being is at peace and is joyful. By choice, they have a cheerful disposition all the time. That way of being started for me on one particular day I remember vividly. I was around the back of our house with my mom and dad. As I watched my mother hand-washing our clothes, it seemed that she was enjoying herself, that she would not rather be anywhere else nor doing anything else. Her contentment, as always, was contagious.

I felt so happy as I breathed in the fresh air and smell of our back yard trees and flowers, mingling with the unforgettable scent of the soap that my mother always used to wash clothes. I felt completely peaceful and serene and I was free of fear and other unwholesome emotions. Though I was quite small, I felt strong. At the time, I could not describe this seed of strength, but I knew it was within me and that no external source was required for contentment as sweet as my mother's—the words I have now are that I somehow knew I could choose to claim my own power. The feeling, the sights, sounds, and smells are indelible in my memory.

The house was the guest house on the property where my father's British boss took residence during his assignment in our region. The day had started with a surprise visit from our cousin. Dad was excited and very happy to see him, so he went and asked his boss if he could spend some time with his cousin and family. His request was granted, making us all happy, as this photograph taken by my cousin shows. In the photo, my dad looks sharp because he always dressed well. That's how he presented himself as he served his boss and the guests of his boss.

To start our impromptu family party, dad changed out of his work clothes and gave our cousin some clothes to put on that were suitable for lounging. Mom finished washing the clothes and started to prepare some *mezethes*. A *meze* is a dish, hot or cold, spicy or savory, often salty, that is served alone or with other *mezethes* as a separate eating experience, sometimes as an appetizer. The role of the *meze* course is two-fold. First, the food is used to complement and enhance the taste of the drink (wines, whiskey, and the like) and second, to provide the backdrop for a social gathering. The little plates are shared by everyone at the table, which not only provides a wonderful variety of flavor and texture sensations but also creates the kind of happy, convivial atmosphere many cultures such as ours are known for.

The scene is so clear in my mind, even today: We are all sitting in the backyard, and the weather is pleasant. I am next to my dad and he has his arm around me. Mom brings the *meza* and they start to drink whisky and to enjoy the tasty food. Everyone is sharing family news and stories of past times together.

I remember feeling so full of contentment, as well as having excited anticipation, waiting for my dad to allow me the tiniest sip of his whiskey.

Soon everyone was singing and laughing, the natural outcome when loved ones are gathered just to celebrate being alive and together—especially with someone like my father around. He was charming and friendly by nature. I consider him my first role model for how to treat people, always managing to help them to feel alive and connected. He would say, "We are Chaldeans," referring to our deep-seated beliefs in hospitality and lovely communal meals.

Suddenly, my dad's boss appeared, walking around the corner of the house and into the backyard. This had never happened before.

It seems he was only curious and my father welcomed him so warmly that he decided to stay and have fun. He started to drink and to sing in English—that is my first memory of hearing English, such a happy time. Mom was already busy preparing more food for our guest, bringing her "A game" by cooking our style of Chaldean food. The party was getting better and better as Dad and my cousin added dance to song. Dad began showing his boss how, as well. Dad swept up my mother to dance, then me, my brother and sister—we were just having a great time! Dinner was served, and Dad's boss went crazy for the food.

He made my dad promise that my mother would cook for him once a week and he would add extra pay into Dad's earnings. I was *experiencing* all of this, and although I was so little, I remember it like it was yesterday.

The evening grew quieter as the night flowers' fragrance grew stronger. It was time to go to sleep and that meant going into the house to bring blankets outside. There was no air conditioning and sleeping outside was the most pleasant experience on earth. Dad insisted that his boss stay and sleep in our backyard and he did! We all slept with only the starlit sky as our roof, blankets on the grass as our bed, and blankets to cover us. This is how I remember learning to count, lying in the back yard, looking up and pointing to each star my father would count for me, 1, 2, 3…

Our beautiful family, our cousin, and my dad's British boss soon fell asleep to the sounds of palm fronds gently catching the fragrant breeze. Every great word one could say about that day would not be enough. Yes, my mind was too young to comprehend everything about the event, but that's not how these memories were formed—the experience was engraved into my soul.

That was the day I realized something—something that would profoundly affect me for the rest of my life. As I said, it was a kind of awakening, an enlightening experience.

That is the day that I came to know that I would never have a bad day in my life.

"Only those who will risk going too far can possibly find out how far one can go."

—**T. S. Eliot**

CHAPTER TWO

My Brave Mother Sets a New Course

After my dad's death, the new home he had just purchased was quickly sold; none of us even got to see it. With my father gone and Saddam Hussein looming larger as our enemy simply because we were not Sunni Arabs, my mother decided we must leave Iraq.

Another reason this felt urgent to her was that I was 17, an age where I could be ordered to join the Iraqi military any day. She became determined to figure out how we could leave, make it to the United States of America, and never return to Iraq.

The first goal was to get to Lebanon, considered at that time as the paradise of the Middle East. We were incredibly fortunate that my mom's brother went to great lengths and expense to help us escape. This uncle arranged everything. My brother-in-law (Rifat) and I left Iraq first because my sister was eight months pregnant and Mom wanted to wait with her until the baby was born.

A few weeks later, Mom and my older sister Basima, with her new baby boy, headed out for Lebanon. Thanks to my beloved uncle's arrangements, Mom was then able to go back to Iraq and bring my other two sisters and my brother Tom to reunite with us in Lebanon.

All of these difficult and risky ordeals were worth it, as my wise mother knew at the time. Iraq was "a living hell," she would say. We left everything behind—our property, friends, relatives, and the place of my father's murder.

Lebanon

We began the task of pulling all of our papers together and creating a file to present to the United States Embassy. We were, again, incredibly fortunate to have a cousin who was living in the US and would sponsor us. I will never forget one piece of advice he gave to me at that time: "Spend all of your money in Lebanon," he said. "In America, money grows on trees." I believed him, literally.

We received our sponsorship papers and were granted a meeting with the embassy. We explained our situation and we were accepted. (I cannot even fathom what a turning point this was in my life.)

We just had to be patient then to receive our visas so we could go. Our financial situation was in decline, so we were forced to move to another less expensive town. We found an apartment within a few weeks.

During one night while we were sleeping, the deafening sound of exploding bombs and other types of weapons woke up the whole family. The civil war in Beirut had started. There was no safety or security for anyone, so everybody who was living in our building ended up in the basement for many days.

The war in Lebanon and the whole situation were just getting worse and worse. We had to move to a different, slightly more secured building. Our whole family of nine people stayed in a small hallway for 17 days!

One night, my brother-in-law and I decided to stretch our legs a bit. We ventured just a few steps down the hallway when all of a sudden, a bomb fell on another building about twenty yards away. The destroyed walls around us sent concrete, wood, and beams flying. My brother-in-law was struck in the neck and I was wounded in the leg. I was so dazed I do not recall how we got there, but we both were admitted into a hospital.

After a few days, a military officer came and spoke with my mom. She told him that we were refugees waiting for our visas. He explained that the war situation would get much worse and asked if we had any relatives who lived nearby, but outside of Beirut.

Mom replied that we had some relatives in Syrian Town and he said arrangements would be made to have a van move us there. As soon as my brother-in-law was recovered enough, we left and found an apartment to rent in Syrian Town (which was in Lebanon, not Syria, but had a large number of Syrian families living there). Finally, after a few months there, we were notified that our visas were ready.

Now we were all in a rush to pack up and leave. The United States, that magical land of our dreams, paid for all of us to fly to Greece and then paid all of our hotel and living expenses for several months while we had to wait for the next step. The Dolphin Hotel-Kalamos was a beautiful resort and we were delighted with the abundance of food—three meals every day plus snacks in between. Greek food is similar to middle-eastern food and we wondered, *if our stop-over place is so heavenly, what must await us when we actually get to America?!*

Coming to America

Our time in Greece was both comfortable and uncomfortable. We were grateful for the safe amount of distance between us and the turmoil we had escaped in Iraq and Lebanon, but we felt unsettled, because we were.

It was exciting and yet surreal when we were notified that arrangements had been made for us to fly to the US, first to New York and then on to Michigan, where our sponsor lived. All concerns about the unknown, all attachments to our vacation resort life in Greece, and all our paralyzing fears about flying across the world quickly vanished. We were ready to begin our new lives.

April 6, 1976: When we arrived, of course there were things that caught us by surprise, but overall, we could not have felt more fortunate. With much gratitude, my mother had us literally kneel and kiss the ground.

We were met at the Detroit Metropolitan Wayne County Airport and greeted by one of our father's closest relatives from Baghdad, who gave us a warm welcome. She was my mother's dearest friend. Her husband had died of cancer in Baghdad, but our family had known him and we sympathized with our aunt because he was a very good man.

She took us to her home where cousins and friends joined us for a wonderful "welcome to America" dinner party. After much celebration, it started getting late and then everyone was getting tired and left. When I woke up the next morning, everything inside and outside looked so different! My whole world had literally changed overnight.

For one thing, this was the first time in my life I had stayed in a wooden house. I went outside to see what everything looked like in the daylight. I looked at all the neighboring homes and sidewalks. White, black, brown… all different types of people lived on the same street, three times wider than our street in Amana. As I watched each passing car, I had to remind myself that indeed, I was now living in this scene! I wasn't watching a movie or dreaming. Everything that I saw, I also could experience. It left me in a state of both awe and gratitude.

One day I asked my cousin out to walk with me around the neighborhood— and especially I wanted him to show me the particular trees where I could pick some dollars. (Yes, *that* cousin.) He agreed and off we went, but he told me to ignore most of the trees because they only had ones and fives— he said we should only look to find the special trees with twenties and hundred-dollar bills. Alas, we didn't see anything but regular trees on the short walk. Later, I found "money trees" to be a metaphor: In America, you can choose to reach for anything...and when you set your mind and efforts toward it, you can attain it.

It was at first puzzling to me to see the "checkerboard" effect where some of the houses, markets, and retail stores were burned down, demolished, or in ruins. I later learned that some inner-city areas had recently endured riots when simmering racial tensions had boiled over. Mobs had actually prevented firefighters from saving burning buildings. Things now seemed settled down, thank goodness.

But the blemishes were far outweighed by the new and wonderful things I was taking in. I learned that relatively speaking, a car, insurance, and gas were much, much cheaper in America.

Actually, I wasn't surprised by anything because I believed America was a magical place.

I had heard that everything was bigger and that everyone had a car. Well, I found out why—nothing was within an easy walking distance! I could hardly wait to own my own car and I wondered how that was going to happen...not if, when!

Michigan Avenue, Detroit, "Motor City" (1976)

48

I still remember many of my first impressions. I had heard that at the neighborhood diner, you could get a second cup of coffee for free. I tried it, and it worked! I also remember being wide-eyed when I saw the portion sizes served in restaurants. Americans seemed to believe "bigger is better" in everything. Even the "open times" of restaurants and shops were extended beyond anything I'd seen before, and many were open seven days a week!

I wasn't used to hearing "thank you" all the time, but that's certainly a typical American habit. I quickly learned that people were friendly, not judgmental, but tended to keep things on more of a superficial level than I was used to. Even after I'd lived here a while, I felt that it wasn't easy to get to really know someone at a deeper level. Everyone would keep a little distance between themselves and others, though not in a rude way. For example, it was strange to me that people's houses did not have fences or walls surrounding them, yet people did not walk onto others' property.

In Iraq and Lebanon, my family was in the minority religiously because we were Christian. In America, churches were on every street and the pre-Christmas hoopla blew my mind. It seemed like everyone had the Christmas spirit. I was already excited since my own birthday is just before Christmas, but the Americans' outdoor house lights, rooftop Santas, and large lit-up trees shining through the windows electrified my sense of wonder.

The thing is that from Day One, I thought of myself as an American. I continued to observe what I was not yet familiar with, soaking up everything like a sponge. Houses made of wood seemed to lack precise engineering, put together every which way. They make up for it in size! Of course, I noticed the American girls, free to wear any style of clothes and apparently free to walk around with and talk with anyone they pleased (with no male relatives keeping close guard). I later learned that you could even ask a girl you did not know to dance and not get shot!

Even though I was a teenager, I had a mature appreciation for this opportunity, this "free country." Remember, my father had been murdered by Iraqi government thugs for the simple reason that he supported different politics. In my new homeland, I was never sent to wait in long lines to purchase eggs and bread. I loved getting to meet people of different nationalities. On my third day in the States, I had an American girlfriend! Honestly, I did not feel homesick then, or ever.

We stayed with our relatives for only a few days. Two blocks down the street, we rented a furnished house. It wasn't long at all before we received welfare funds from the government to help with our living expenses. This was a low-income part of Detroit and most people were on welfare.

Chico Tries it All

I said to myself, *wow, I'm really here…here in America, where the sky's the limit!* I believed with such conviction that doors of opportunity would fly open at any moment, and I didn't have long to wait. An Iraqi man knocked on our door. He had heard that we just arrived and explained that he was one of the large Chaldean family who owned the Sheraton Hotel where my father had worked in Baghdad. In addition to welcoming us, he offered me work in his grocery market. Perfect! On my third day in America, I was employed! My schedule was six days a week, from 9 a.m. to 9 p.m. I was thanking God that I gotten a job without knowing how to speak, read, or write English and received $60 per week, which I thought was fantastic.

But working there was far from idyllic. In the heart of a dangerous neighborhood, we had to always be on guard. The store was robbed many times. Inside, the owner and one cashier remained behind the counter with a bulletproof shield at all times. I was always walking back and forth from the back storage area to the aisles and shelves of the store, as it was my job to keep everything well-stocked. It's a good thing I'm not color-blind, because that is the only way I could determine what went where. Not knowing how to read any of the stickers or labels, I had to look at the colors and images to stock everything.

I started paying attention when my boss communicated with the customers, and I began picking up few words. I was practicing my pronunciation and growing vocabulary. I learned all beverages' tastes and their names, especially alcoholic beverages. I stayed at this store for a couple of months, then was offered a better position in a different, bigger market with better security and security guards. I was paid more money there—90 dollars per week for fewer hours, working from 10 a.m. to 6 p.m., six days a week.

It felt like I was finally having some time for myself. We moved to another, slightly better house. My brother got a job at Chrysler, and THAT was a big deal. Our financial situation was quickly improving. Then my brother got married and moved out. I was starting to mingle more, my social life greatly influenced by whom I already knew, my cousins.

I loved hanging out with my cousin and one day we visited a bar that had live entertainment. I fell in love with this bar and its rock-n-roll bands. My cousin had long hair, just like most everyone else at that time. Mine was not quite so long—in fact, everybody at the bar called me "Chico" from the very popular TV show *Chico and the Man*. I saw an episode, and yes, I guess I did look like Chico (Freddie Prinze) with my thick dark hair and mustache. I loved having a nickname and the opportunity to socialize more and more with English-speaking peers.

As my English improved, I felt confident enough to start talking with girls and dating for the first time in my life. Life was getting more interesting every day and I started making even more money with my job. After one year in Detroit, we moved to Warren city, into a nicer home and area. After only eighteen months, that landlord told us that we had to move out because he planned to demolish the house and add a mini-mart to his liquor store. So we moved out and went back to Detroit, but this time to a much better neighborhood.

This was my favorite house; it felt very cozy and warm, and Mom loved it. Now, if only I could achieve the American teenager's dream…I decided I had to have a car and, still intoxicated with my belief that "anything is possible in America," I knew I would (somehow) soon be driving one.

And so I bought my first car in early 1977, paying the $700 purchase price over time, $50 a month to my brother-in-law who was kind enough to extend me the credit. Ah, what a beauty! A 1967 Chevrolet Impala, honey brown in color. Time to learn how to drive!

Wouldn't I love to still have my first car! ('67 Impala, very similar to above)

We were always among minorities and lower-income neighbors and having a car was a big deal. I would drive it everywhere, even when the walk would have been easy. On my way to work, I would drive by the arcade, showing off to my friends. There were always people hanging out there, mostly young men like me, between 18 and 20, a few younger or older. It was very social and loosely organized around playing video games, billiards, darts, ping pong, and pinball.

The arcade was the most diverse watering hole you can imagine: all types of nationalities including Chaldeans, Albanians, Assyrians, and American Blacks, Hispanics, and whites. I was impressed that everyone easily mingled and spoke in English to one another. Even if someone from, say, Albania, had been in America 10 years, I felt like I should be able to speak English as well as they did. Since *anything* was possible in America, I was confident that I soon would be fluent in English. At the arcade, I started seriously practicing my English. Every time I used a new word, it felt like a small victory on my way to great things ahead.

Friday nights and weekends were very busy at the arcade and I was a regular. I was on top of the world: my own nice-looking car, a steady job, nice clothes, and a very popular look at the time (long, unruly hair and a thick mustache). A confident, happy young person is automatically attractive and popular: I had a beautiful girlfriend and plenty of new friends who seemed to especially enjoy introducing me to their favorite pastimes like rock-n-roll, weed, Colt 45 malt liquor, and Mad Dog 20/20. I'd had high expectations of life in America and everything seemed to be even better than I imagined. I told my mother, "I want to live the American way and marry an American girl." (That eventually worked out wonderfully—married 42 years, and still going strong!)

One day, my brother-in-law came to the house and told me to get ready because we were going to apply to work at "Ford" and that we were "going to make lots of money." We got the job!

The company which hired us was actually called "Bradford Production." They specialized in making parts for the Ford Motor Company. Our work schedule was five days, 7 a.m.–3 p.m. shifts. Overtime and weekend work was optional and I took advantage of that. It was so fun to have my own money to spend at the arcade or a bar. My favorite club was Clark Gable's on the west side, but I said to myself one day, *I am going to drive over to the east side.*

I did that because one of my cousins recommended this place on the east side and told me its location. I had no idea what this club was all about, but I drove into the east side to check it out. I stopped to park the car, and they refused to let me in because I wasn't dressed properly (jeans, t-shirt, jacket, and boots). I explained that I just came to see what it looked like; I just needed to park for five minutes and check inside, and I would leave immediately. Somehow, I managed to convince them and my trip to the east side was not wasted. It was my first of a million times to that bar. I had the fever.

The next day, I visited my cousin's hair salon because I wanted the same haircut as I'd seen on most men in that club. She did a phenomenal job. She said, "Well, now you look just like John Travolta!" I trimmed my mustache as well. I drove to the mall to buy myself new suits, ties, shirts, and shoes. I could hardly wait for the bar to open that night.

I put on my new clothes and shoes, admiring my "total look" including my new hairstyle. I came out of my room and when my mother saw me, she started to cry. She said that my father used to dress like that all the time. I started to cry as well, wishing that Dad was there to see me dressed like him, making my way, and loving life.

"When you dance, you can enjoy
the luxury of being you."

—Paulo Coelho

CHAPTER THREE

Saturday Night Fever

Dance transcends all language, cultural, and ethnic barriers. I believe it to be humanity's first and everlasting expression of soul.

"To dance is to be out of yourself. Larger, more beautiful, more powerful... This is power, it is glory on earth and it is yours for the taking." —Agnes De Mille.

It's hard to describe how I felt walking into the club that first night with my Travolta persona. It was like heaven for me—a scene from *Saturday Night Fever*, but real! I loved it so much and felt like I owned the world. All the ladies had lovely hairstyles, wore gorgeous nightclub dresses, and most of the dancers were professionals. I sat at a table sipping a drink and watched the amazing dancers for hours. I kept watching how their feet were moving. I went to the east side club three nights in a row, strictly as an observer.

The Eastern Swing was the first dance I decided I wanted to master. I practiced, even while I was at work. On the fourth day, when I went back to the bar, it was my first time asking someone to dance without fear. I asked one of the dancers, and she accepted, but she knew right away that I wasn't a good dancer when I started to dance. I know that because when I asked her again to dance, she rejected me. I confirmed to myself that it's all well and that I will become a great dancer one day.

The name of the club was "Butterfly" and I kept visiting the club regularly. Unless I was with my family, my communication (using English) was still very limited and limiting. Fully expressing myself was not yet possible, except when I was dancing at the club.

"You dance love, and you dance joy, and you dance dreams. And I know if I can make you smile by jumping over a couple of couches or running through a rainstorm, then I'll be very glad to be a song and dance man."

—Gene Kelly

Despite my broken English, I met many new friends. My joy in dancing and my stylish look indeed helped a lot. I was intent on not just being a good dancer having fun, I truly wanted to become a great dancer, learning ballroom dancing steps as well as modern dance. It was a challenge, as it seemed that my body moved differently than anyone else. I was undeterred and practiced constantly.

One day a dancer friend said that there was another new club called Carmen East in the same area. I checked it out and was fascinated with it. I met the club owner, and he would always shake my hand because I was bringing so much business to his club! I was getting popular thanks to my dancing skills, which were getting better every day. Many dancers followed me to whatever club I patronized.

One night, I heard the news that a major dance competition was coming up. My favorite dance partner was with me that night at Carmen East and we decided right then to sign up together for the contest. A few doubts about being ready? Sure, but my choice was to go for it! Since it would be held at the Rare Cherry, we started frequenting that bar so we would be familiar with their dance floor.

Round-the-clock practice for disco dance competitions

Every time I made up a new move, I immediately called my dance partner and we met at the club. We practiced a lot to help our chances in this statewide contest, with 372 couples competing. All of the other contestants were professional dancers. The contests for this phase were spread out, held in different clubs. Our event was at the Rare Cherry and we won first place!

Right after we were announced as winners, I saw a beautiful blond walking toward the exit door, leaving the club. I had never seen her at the club before and had no idea who she was, but I sure hoped she'd return.

The following week, my dance partner and I went to the next level of the competition, which was held at Carmen East—and we won again! I was starting to feel like a celebrity! The final competition would be held at the Renaissance Center in downtown Detroit, an impressive, new, towering glass and steel architectural wonder at that time.

The competition had been narrowed down to only six couples remaining out of 372 couples. We had three weeks to choose a new song, create our dance plan, and practice.

As finalists, my dance partner and I were extremely busy being interviewed on every news channel. I tried my best to speak in my broken English so they could understand me, but I knew I wasn't there for much talk but to give a short dance performance with my partner. In addition to TV, we were featured in newspapers and other media. Incredibly, my name became well-known in the state of Michigan.

Finally, the day came for the final competition. I felt on top of the world. I was not nervous, just very excited. My partner and I walked into the beautiful Renaissance Center. Hundreds of people crowded the lobby, but we spotted our "fan" group including my brother, sister-in-law, other relatives, and many, many friends.

We had practiced together every free minute and felt very prepared. But we were not prepared in one critical respect—we were supposed to bring a record album of our music we would be dancing to in the contest. In all the excitement, my partner forgot to bring our record. We checked with the DJ. He didn't have our music, but provided a similar song (one by Cher).

All the finalist couples were excited but also nervous because the stage seemed so huge, the audience was so pumped up, and there was a big-name band playing that night. Each couple was called in turn to come up onto the stage as the audience clapped and cheered enthusiastically for everyone.

My partner and I were called after the first two couples. We wore very sharp, coordinated outfits, mine a tuxedo, hers a shiny white dress. The minute we stepped onto the stage's dance floor, the audience went crazy.

The song started and I was dancing just for that moment, not worrying about winning. I felt like I was in heaven and that the world belonged to me. The joy and happiness I felt couldn't be exchanged for anything in the world.

In what seemed like seconds later, our dance was over and we went to wait breathlessly in the wings until all the contestants had danced. The band played while the judges convened and then finally it was time to announce the winner. Number one in the state of Michigan—first place—went to my partner and me! We won a three-day trip to Florida, but the greatest reward for me was knowing I had achieved the goal I had worked for and believed in.

Across the state, people who followed the competition were stunned. My partner and I were the only amateurs in the competition, the rest were all professionals. I had started dancing less than one year before this contest. I was super happy, but not incredulous—because anything is possible in America!

Marilyn Monroe Changes Everything

There was much celebration that night with friends and relatives. A week later, the club owner organized a big party. Drinking and living it up, I suddenly had the urge to turn around and look at the entrance door. There she was. The love of my life walked into the club. Of course, everybody was staring at her. When she got close, I couldn't help but think of Marilyn Monroe. I vividly recalled the time when at a very young age I'd told my father that some day I would marry my own Marilyn Monroe.

I called the waiter over and asked him to take a bottle of champagne to the blonde's table across the room and tell her it was from me. Then I asked the DJ to play my favorite song and I dedicated a special dance just for her. After dancing, I went to her table to introduce myself and at the same moment, I knew that there really is something to "love at first sight." I asked her name—just hearing her voice saying her beautiful name "Sheri" made my heart stop.

It was near closing time and many of us usually went to another bar that stayed open later. I asked her to follow me, and she agreed. But her two friends wanted to go home so she couldn't just abandon them, and she felt bad. The very next day, she came to the club with a carnation, which she gave to me, giving me an innocent kiss on the cheek. At that moment, millions of thoughts raced through my mind: Marilyn Monroe, my father, the state championship, and what it felt like looking into the eyes of the most beautiful woman in the world.

On my first date with Sheri, I was between cars and had to borrow my brother's van to use. Now, this was a true 70s van. It was typical to have a custom paint job and an abundance of stickers, each reflecting the personality and interests of the owner. My brother's van was the craziest one—it had women's titties, snakes, scales—all kind of weird stuff was on it. But I did not care how I got there; I was ecstatic to be on my way to pick up my dream girl.

I knocked on the door and my future mother-in-law opened it. Of course, I was very excited as she greeted me and asked me to enter. My future father-in-law was in his favorite La-Z-Boy chair. I walked over to him and shook his hand, praying that he would not start any conversation with me and force me to struggle along in my broken English.

When he got up and looked outside, he saw the van and I thought he was going to kick me out right then. He managed to react only with a little laugh and commented on what his daughter "has brought home this time." Thank God I survived.

We started driving towards the restaurant. The only reason I liked going to that particular restaurant was that they had a menu with pictures on it, which was easy for me as I would just point my finger at a meal I wanted. We had a great dinner, and then we went to my house so my mother could meet her. When mom saw her, she was shocked for few seconds and then she welcomed her in. The whole family came and sat, staring at Sheri. Mom was amazed, thinking she looked like a beautiful doll. She later told me that she remembered the day I had told my dad that I would marry a "Marilyn" one day.

Soon it was time for my dance partner and I to head to Florida to compete in the National Championship. Everything was paid for us. We were so excited and had a great time. After our late breakfast, we did some practice and started drinking. We kept drinking and decided to go by the pool and lay in the sun. We both fell asleep in the hot sun, and when we woke up, we could hardly move. Our Michigan skin wasn't used to the Florida sun, and we both ended up in the hospital with a severe sunburn. We lost the opportunity to compete in the National Championship and came back to Michigan very disappointed. I knew in my heart that I was going to win the Nationals. I guess it wasn't meant to be.

"The only way to make sense out of change is to plunge into it, move with it, and join the dance."

—Alan Watts

CHAPTER FOUR

Move to California

Sheri became my girlfriend. We started discussing our future, my dancing career, and her modeling career. California (especially Hollywood) was considered *the* entertainment capital at that time. Suddenly, I decided to go ahead and move to California. I did not have even enough funds for a plane ticket, but I was determined to head to the Golden State.

Thank goodness Sheri was in total agreement. She also did not have money to make the trip to California, but she sold a ring in order to get a ticket and follow her dream. She had the good fortune of having an old friend from school already there, living in Anaheim. Sheri left for the West Coast, stayed with her friend, and waited for me.

I didn't have any fear; I was full of confidence and courage. I told myself that if I had managed to accomplish so much in Michigan in a very short period, I could do the same in California. I was amazed at the time to learn that the state of California is nearly the same size in square miles as the entire country of Iraq! I managed to convince my mother to let me go with her blessing, promising her that I would move the entire family there if everything worked out well.

I had a cousin living in Anaheim, the same area where Sheri lived, and he opened his doors to me. My brother helped me in purchasing a ticket, so I finally said goodbye to Michigan.

One huge benefit, by the way, of living with The 5 Cornerstone Choices is that when you feel your heart urging you to make a big change in your life, you'll find the the courage to do it.

Set'n Style YOUR HAIR

100s of Great New Looks for Your Hair

THAT YOU CREATE YOURSELF!

BUSY GIRL CUTS FOR NIGHT & DAY

SULTRY-LOOKING STYLES TO CAPTIVATE YOUR MAN!

EASY STYLING TRICKS THAT WORK LIKE MAGIC!

SIMPLE-TO-FOLLOW SETTING PATTERNS

CHARLEY'S Hair Design   481-8762
2540 Cottage Way, Sacramento
Hair & Make-up: Rodert Dickson
Photo: Focuses   Model: Sheri Soro

California modeling welcomed Sheri with open arms!

Sheri started modeling for an agency and I began dancing. At the same time, we both worked unglamorous jobs (which we were happy to have). I painted apartment buildings. I was also improving my dance skills and doing great. Sheri suggested that I sign up with a famous dance studio in Hollywood, which many movie stars also attended. I accepted her advice, and I was doing very well.

Full of joy, I called my mother to invite her to move to California. She moved there, along with with my two sisters, Kelly and Rita, and my brother, Tom. They all stayed with Sheri and me in a two-bedroom apartment in the city of Fullerton. We knew that was temporary, but worth it to all be together.

I somehow managed to juggle my work, family, love life, dance studio time, and my preparation for a dance competition— and everybody seemed to be very happy. There was always a dance competition happening at one nightclub or another, as these were always sure to draw customers.

My uncle, who was my best friend, arrived from Iraq. I was so thrilled to see the person I had learned so much from in my youth and loved being around. The apartment was then too small to accommodate all of us, so we decided to move to a house. One day, I don't really know what happened to me, but I just didn't want to dance anymore. I asked Sheri to leave her modeling career, plan to marry me, and have a family. She accepted my proposal for our future and we waited for a while to make a set plan.

Whenever I was low on cash, I would compete and win some money.

Sheri and I as winning dance partners

I started to get tired of painting, probably because it was too much of a solo job..I needed people connection! I attended a 12-week program at a bartending school, but I finished it earlier—in only two weeks. My instructor could not believe I had never before bartended. The only bartending experience I had was with my father in Baghdad, but there was no such thing as mixing drinks there because we were selling everything in bottles.

My brother decided to come out West from Michigan as well, and he immediately started to look for a business to purchase after his arrival. There was a cleaning business for sale for a very reasonable price, and he bought it. My whole family was working there; they cleaned houses, office buildings, and apartments. The business was quickly growing and everyone felt more secure than we had in a long time.

I asked Sheri to marry me on Valentine's Day, 1980, and we got married August 23, 1980. Our wedding was very special because the Chaldean patriarch conducted our ceremony. That is very honorable in our culture because this is considered very special treatment.

Our Blessed Marriage (August 23, 1980)

My vision had brought me Sheri, and I knew that for the rest of our lives, I would honor her and continue to give her special treatment. This intention has been my north star for over four decades and has everything to do with me being able to say that *I've never had a bad day in my life.*

"Life is the dancer and you are the dance."

—Eckhart Tolle

CHAPTER FIVE

As Luck Would Have It

"You are so lucky!" My friend was sincerely happy for me about something that happened—I don't recall what. What I do remember is that something about what he said just didn't feel right. Frankly, I knew that it was a lie.

Much later, I heard a definition for "luck" that had a ring of truth:

Luck is what happens where preparation meets opportunity.

One significant benefit of making The 5 Cornerstone Choices is that you become as prepared as you possibly could be for a door of opportunity to appear and present you with a choice to make. This is how the fundamental 5 Cornerstone Choices guarantee that you will have more, and more, and more choices in your life! This is the definition of freedom.

"Freedom is the oxygen of the soul."

—Moshe Dayan

We received an offer and opportunity to sell our cleaning business. As "luck" would have it, I was at the same time offered an excellent bartending position in Sacramento, California. So we made the choice to sell it and to move to Sacramento. My brother moved to Turlock, California. I had a cousin living in the city of Carmichael and he invited us in to stay with them for a while.

Hospitality: I Am My Father's Son

I grew up in the hospitality business, watching and helping my dad, a true master. He had a natural gift and I seemed to have inherited his aptitude and, most importantly, enthusiasm for the challenge of providing remarkable service. It turned out to be the perfect career for a people-oriented person like myself.

As with The 5 Cornerstone Choices, your level of intentionality and focus on what's important has everything to do with your success—in life or in any career. The hospitality business has a great mission, don't you agree? That is, do whatever it takes to make guests and customers feel comfortable, and make their experience enjoyable. My life revolved around this *commitment to caring* for many decades. I'll share here a few of the principles that my dad taught me by being a role model, and that I later learned to distinguish, consistently implement, and teach to others:

- First impressions count so much—ensure each guest or customer recieves a friendly, warm welcome. This puts them at ease. Also, they will feel appreciated and eager to return if they are warmly acknowledged as they leave.

- One should be knowledgeable and not only know how to answer questions, but also anticipate what would be helpful to tell a customer. All communication to guests should be purposeful, patient, and never intrusive.

- Always look at things from the guest's perspective. Are employees rushing around, lazing around, or looking disorganized? Or does it look like everyone is on the ball and enjoying their work and customers?

- The best establishments are not stuck on rules as much as they are bound by their mission to serve. A customer might ask for something not listed on the menu, for example, but if a new combination can be created for them, why not make them happy?

- When a guest experiences consistent, warm hospitality, there is a bond of trust established that is priceless to the establishment. No clever advertising or famous chef can match that for gaining popularity and success.

- Masters of hospitality—including managers, bartenders, servers, hostesses, or valets, to name a few—are always seeking ways to improve the guests' experience. Little touches, such as recalling a guest's name or offering a coloring page to a child are sure to be remembered. People don't forget a time when a manager gave them a complimentary appetizer or glass of wine because of a delay or mistake.

Serving Others Served My Family and Me Very Well

Two weeks after starting my new job, we rented a place and moved out from my cousin's. As a bartender, my shift was from 9 p.m. to 2 a.m., Wednesday to Sunday. I got another job at a country club as an assistant waiter. I worked hard and took good care of the family. The next month, through someone I met at the club, I was offered a head bartender position in a very famous Greek restaurant, "Zorba's."

When I say "very famous,"I mean this place was known far and wide, not just in California. It is a wonderful success story of a man, Nick Galazidas, who immigrated from Greece to Bolivia, then to Canada where he found work as a restaurant dishwasher. He worked his way up and later moved to California, near his wife's family in Sacramento. He worked at several local restaurants, and in 1966 he took over the Golden Slipper, the future home of Zorba the Greek.

He became the owner in 1967 and gradually built the business from an "empty basement" to one of Sacramento's most popular restaurants/nightclubs. Nick became the host known for his warmth and friendliness, and as an entertainer as well. Many people came just to see him do his famous Ouzo Tavern Dance in which he lifted a heavy table with his teeth, dancing all the while.

Nick Galazidas, famous for his Greek restaurant and entertainment, including lifting a table with his teeth during the Ouzo Tavern Dance. Background, right, me doing traditional Greek dance. OPA! (1981)

Yes, I saw this with my own eyes. In fact, once I saw him do this while a woman belly-danced on top of the table!

All the dancing, hospitality, and booming business made me count my blessings every day that I had found this opportunity that suited me so well. The club expanded and booked big-name entertainers to perform. People would stand in the aisles—anything to get into this place. I danced the Greek dances like you've see a line of men doing. One time I got to dance with Anthony Quinn who was paying a visit to Zorba the Greek's. (Of course, Quinn was in the film, *Zorba the Greek*, back in 1964, and was nominated for Best Actor.)

The Greek restaurant was so much fun, life felt great, and these are lovely memories. After one year, my first child, Dylan, was born, another precious addition to my blessed life.

To Everything There is a Season

I have a saying that I use as a reminder to myself as well as to share with others: *This too shall pass.* When things have taken a downturn and life feels hard and joyless, I promise you this is only temporary. Conversely, when things are flying high and all seems fantastic, change is inevitable. This too shall pass. The best use of this universal truth is to stay optimistic and hopeful when the chips are down, and when things are wonderful, breathe it all in with deep gratitude. And so, as wildly successful and enjoyable as Nick's restaurant was, its vibrant life came to an end when Nick decided to retire.

He just started getting tired after so many years. He used to dance two shows every day and of course he became so well-known for the feat, he was expected to do the table-lifting performances every day. In 1983, Nick retired from performing and also closed the restaurant. He and his restaurant remain a fond memory for thousands of people, including myself.

I did not want to be out of work, so when Nick's friend offered me a day-shift bartending job, I accepted. The atmosphere there could not have been more different from the raucous times at Zorba's. The restaurant was exquisite and upscale, specializing in what the French call "flambé" cuisine. The culinary technique flambé (flahm-BAY) shares the same origin as the word flamboyant. A hallmark of old-school fine dining, a dish prepared *en flambé* is traditionally done tableside by waiters sporting tuxedos. Although it looks like your food is on fire, it's really just the added alcohol burning off, leaving nothing behind but pure flavor without the sharp bite of the booze. It's both for show and cuisine excellence, if done correctly.

I thought the place was very nice, but my lounge was almost always empty! I began to wonder why. I was told that since they opened the restaurant, the business had never picked up. I took this as a challenge! I set out to prove what I could do over the next three months.

I knew that the excellent food, location, and abundance of local wealthy clientele were all to the restaurant's distinct advantage. But the place didn't have any "personality." I made it my job to warm the place up. I always asked each and every guest that walked in for their name, for example. Gradually, the lounge started getting busy. My boss was happy, and he wanted me to do the same thing in the dining room.

Enjoying myself and having fun was
always contagious to customers (1983)

The dining room was very elegant, with a formal setting and service. All waiters were dressed in tuxedos and my boss was always wearing a suit. Many of our wealthy guests had their own driver and limousine, attracted to the restaurant because of the elegance and VIP service. Some of the waiters stayed there for years. The difference between them and me was that I loved the business, which they didn't. They were just coming there to collect their tips and go home, but I was different.

71

I always asked for guests' last names and I memorized these; the guests loved it when they came again. They started asking for me when booking a reservation. I was fully booked from Wednesday to Sunday. My tips were between $1100 to $1500 a night, and this was in the early 80's. I was awarded the Best Waiter of the Year and Best Flambé Captain in the dining room. At that time, I considered myself the best *maître de* ANYwhere, even though my English was something I was still working on.

I also became very close to one of my guests, who was very wealthy and whose family controlled 70% of the steel business in Sacramento. Many times they would wait until I finished my shift and invite me to follow them to their house for a party. The man seemed to be a great guy, husband, and father of three. He asked me why my wife and I were still living in the apartment. I told him the truth, that it was due to financial issues.

One day he asked me to visit his company to check it out. He took me on tour and the place was amazing, with more than two hundred employees. When I was getting ready to leave, he handed me an envelope and told me to promise him I would not open it until I got home and could open it together with Sheri. When we opened the envelope, inside was a 16-thousand-dollar check, written for a down payment on a house!

Sheri and I started looking for a home, but unfortunately, we couldn't qualify because I wasn't showing enough steady income to make the mortgage. I went back to his house and returned the check to him. I told him why and he offered more help, but I declined and told him it wasn't meant to be. I felt disappointed for about one minute. To everything there is a season...If one door closes, when you live consistent with The 5 Cornerstone Choices, you just know that another opportunity of choice is already on its way to you.

One day I saw one of my friends who I used to work with at the Greek restaurant and he asked me if I could get him a waiter position. I asked my boss if we could squeeze him in, and he gave him a job. My mother never trusted this guy, but because of my ignorance, I disagreed with her. He witnessed my success at the restaurant and after some time, he wanted to taste it. He turned his back against me, lied, and told my boss that I was doing drugs. This went on for a while; it was not good for the restaurant's reputation, but I had no clue. One day my boss fired me.

A mile away from that establishment was another lovely restaurant owned by a chef from India who was married to an English woman. I applied, and he hired me immediately. The restaurant did not have flambé, but I shared my enthusiasm for this special enhancement for atmosphere and cuisine and persuaded him to invest in cooking carts.

Gradually, most of my customers from the previous restaurant started to follow me. After a few months, my old boss apologized to me and asked me to come back. I returned because I loved that place and I didn't care that much about my so-called friend, who I don't like to call "friend" anymore. My mother was right about him; he was an evil snake.

I did not think I could make more money anywhere else in the area and I was set on saving enough to get a home for us with no problems. But as we saved our funds, Sheri started to miss her parents and family even more than longing for our own house. It was understandable, especially since we had little Dylan and they had never even seen him, their first grandchild. We talked about it, and Sheri convinced me to go back to Michigan and live there.

"Life is either a daring adventure, or nothing."

—Helen Keller

CHAPTER SIX

A New Michigan Adventure

Sheri and I went back to Michigan and lived with my in-laws in the city of Warren, near 8 Mile Road (the area which later became a movie based on famed rapper Eminem growing up there). I bought myself an old BMW to drive around. I got a job at Hotel San Regis in downtown Detroit, opposite the headquarters of General Motors. The hotel connected to a large performance venue, the Fisher building, where the majority of Detroit's special events and concerts were taking place. Guests would stay at the hotel, have a nice dinner, and then walk through to the Fisher building to see a show—an especially wonderful arrangement during snow storms!

I was the dining room flambé captain of this beautiful Victorian-style hotel building in an England-themed setting. My customers were movie stars, high-ranking politicians, sports icons and other celebrities. I was inspired to become someone well-known for extraordinary service with style. Soon, I was doing very well financially.

Dylan was getting ready to start school. Sheri and I preferred for him to go to school outside Warren, so we decided to move several miles away to 16 Mile Big Beaver Road in the city of Troy, a developing area with high-rise buildings going up at every turn. The rent ($800 a month) was nearly three times higher in Troy than in Warren, but we were confident that our move would give Dylan a safer neighborhood and better education. It took me more time to drive to work, but I was counting my blessings that I had a great job, a wonderful wife and son, and a nice school and neighborhood for us to enjoy.

A Life-Affirming "Golden Pen"

One day, a family of five came into the hotel and had dinner at the restaurant. They were so pleased with my service that they told me I must come and work for them! They offered me the job of dining room manager at the Kingsley Inn in the city of Bloomfield Hills. They promised me that they would be more than happy to double my salary. Every politician, celebrity, and movie star stayed at the Kingsley, and no expense was spared for top-tier excellence in all regards.

Of course, I accepted the offer and felt fortunate that along with a significant income boost, this new job was located much closer to where we lived— only six minutes from my house. No one realized how much I lacked in being able to read or write in English, but I suppose I spoke well enough. I managed to provide an excellent living for my family and me.

The owner of the Kingsley Inn appreciated me and took good care of me. I learned what it feels like to have someone see your potential and believe in you. He received an offer from the Dale Carnegie motivational seminar company and he insisted that I go and take the course, which lasted for 12 weeks.

Everyone in that class was a professional. I had no idea what was going on and skipped all of the workbook studies. However, every week we were given two minutes in which to give an impromptu speech. Everyone liked me and I was chosen as the best speaker in the class. At the end of the course, I won a golden pen as a present.

Later in my life, I reflected on my Dale Carnegie experience with some amazement. Curious, I went to their web site and learned that "the prestigious Dale Carnegie Course Highest Award for Achievement is awarded based on peer-voting. Peers elect the individual who best exemplifies the standards, qualities and consistent practice of the Human Relations Principles on which the program is based." The winner, to this day, gets a golden pen.

Someone told me that I "speak from the heart" and I have to imagine that is true, since I never gave a speech using prepared or memorized notes. This is a perfect example of what unpredictable and wonderful outcomes can happen when you "Choose to Be Yourself."

Birth

My wife and I were excited to learn that we would be expecting our second child. Sheri asked me to promise that I would accompany her in the delivery room to help her ease her pain because I had not been able to do it with Dylan. My mother was there, too. I was sitting next to Sheri, holding her hands, but when she told me, "Honey, I don't feel well..." I passed out. The staff left Sheri since they had to take care of me. Looking back, we think it was hilarious! In the end, Derek was born very healthy, and Sheri was well.

I enjoyed my work at the Inn, but with a growing family, I was open to bigger opportunities. My uncle from California wanted to start a business with me, although he had no experience. He came to stay with us while we explored possibilities, agreeing that a restaurant would make the best business choice because of my background. He paid for commercial rent and we started working together.

As with anything I decided to take on, I felt I must be 100% committed and give the business my full attention and effort. I was working seven days a week from 7 a.m. to 9 p.m., but by the time we finished the cleaning and some preparations for the next day, we seldom left the restaurant until after 10 or 11 p.m. That was my life.

Sheri got pregnant with Ashley, but I was exhausting myself and lost 40 pounds. Sheri would have appreciated my help with our two boys and with her needs as a tired and pregnant mother. Understandably, she was not happy that I seemed to never be home. I knew it was time for me to make a change. I didn't have to stay in a role that conflicted with my priorities of being there for my family—I could make a different choice, and I did. The fast decision meant walking away from the restaurant with no money, but my uncle understood why I had to leave. (He partnered with another relative of ours who had restaurant experience.)

I set out to look for another job and soon found an opportunity to work for a country club in South Lyon, Michigan. The club offered me the position of dining room manager. It was a private club, with close to 500 very affluent members. Because the same clientele came every day, it wasn't long before I knew everybody's name. Managing the entire dining room meant that I could attend to every guest, at least to briefly greet them or ask if they were enjoying everything, rather than only having a few tables of customers as a server.

I had to drive an hour each way, but I was happy doing it. All the members liked me and showed me respect, and it was mutual. They knew that Sheri was pregnant and often inquired as to how she was doing. When Sheri gave birth to our daughter at the hospital in Sterling Heights, many members sent presents for beautiful baby Ashley. There were so many presents that we were not able to fit everything in Sheri's hospital room.

Back on the job after two days, I was working at the club when the bartender called me over to pick up a phone call. It was the hospital letting me know that Ashley needed to be moved to another hospital. When I heard that, my heart stopped and I couldn't feel my legs. Ashley was transferred from Sterling Heights to downtown Detroit Children's Hospital. My employer and customers instantly understood that I had to leave. I drove about one hundred miles an hour to the downtown hospital. I didn't want Ashley to be there alone.

My baby was in a small rectangular box, her breathing seemed difficult, and it was driving me crazy. I sat next to her, as close as possible, for the next seven hours, longing to hold her. The pediatrician finally told me that she was improving. Ashley stayed in the hospital two more days, though Sheri went home and I went back to work. All the club members were concerned and worried about Ashley. We were told she was completely recovered and we took our baby home.

I found it very touching that the members and my coworkers were so genuinely concerned and were all pulling for us. Years later, when I would have my own employees, I always remembered that each of them is an individual person with cares and concerns outside of work. This is key to building a mutually beneficial relationship. When my own family concerns loomed so large, I felt like I had the support of a large extended family, the Walnut Creek Country Club.

Usually, the club was closed during the winter season in January, February, and March. Rather than risk me finding employment elsewhere and not returning, they offered to pay me for those three months to assure I would be there when they reopened. One of the members asked me what I was going to do during those three months. I said I would love to go to a college. He turned out to be a community college director, and he arranged for me to meet with someone in Admissions. I was so excited!

I signed up to study Business Administration, with a specialization in the hospitality field, including food, beverage, and labor cost control. Unlike the last time I was in a classroom as a child, I was excited on my first day because I believed that what I was to learn would be practical and useful to me and my family. The professor began teaching his material and I was stunned. I had no idea what he was talking about. He spoke so fast and I couldn't keep up with him.

I went back home very disappointed and told Sheri the situation. She suggested that I use a recorder in classes to keep up. I knew this was a good idea because English was my major challenge, so I only slept three hours a day. Sheri and my uncle helped me with my English. Initially, there were 56 students, and I was the oldest one. At the end of the course, only six students completed the course and I was among them. When I brought home my course completion certificate (with my "C" grade), I was really excited. I put it on the refrigerator door like a proud parent would do.

Spring and New Beginnings

When the club opened again that spring, I started back to work. Each time a member would come in, it was like a happy reunion. What a wonderful feeling to know that you are working where you are appreciated. One day, a member asked me a question and it resulted in my whole life trajectory dramatically changing.

He simply asked me if I could replace mayonnaise with a healthier version for sandwiches and toppings. I made him a serving of hummus with dill and he loved it. Soon, everyone wanted hummus with dill. Then I started making a roasted pepper hummus and the members loved it, too. All of a sudden, everyone was talking about "hummus" and back then, almost no one had ever heard the word before.

I loved the fact that I had independently found a way to use my creativity and commitment to service to produce something that was so valued. When the house directly across from the club was put up for sale, the Board of Directors decided to purchase it and let me and my family live in it. They said it would be like I was keeping an eye on the club, but mainly they wanted to strengthen my ties to my employer. This sounded wonderful to Sheri and she was very excited. Sometimes a wonderful offer has strings attached which must be considered. As I was considering this offer/opportunity/commitment, a very different option presented itself.

My cousin had a restaurant that was limping along, despite its excellent 100% Middle-Eastern cuisine. He believed that I could turn it around and offered me 50% ownership, and I accepted. Sheri wasn't glad about the decision. I tend to always want to explore things I have never experienced before.

The overwhelming success of my hummus creations was on the top of my mind and I quickly realized that my cousin's place would provide the location I needed to pursue my ideas. I had made the two different hummus styles and all the club members had enjoyed it—I just knew it would be a gold mine to serve the public. I only needed a location to mass-produce it and sell it to retail stores. My cousin's timing was perfect and I took over the restaurant. I had never seen such a poorly patronized restaurant—slow lunch and slow dinner, too—but I admit it was not in a good location at all. I set to work to make improvements that I knew would help.

I changed the menu to 50% Middle-Eastern and the other 50% French and Italian. I asked my carpenter friend to build cooking carts for me to start offering flambé preparation at diners' tables. I trained the servers and they were all outfitted in tuxedos. I started advertising and we were becoming busy. Very busy.

It's an incredible feeling when your heavy concentration of effort at the beginning of a project starts to gain traction and then momentum. In this endeavor, I was especially motivated because for the first time, I had ownership and felt that each success was stacking up, building something substantial for me and my family. My partner promised me that his handshake was as good as gold, and he swore to God that I was in for 50%. No documents. I trusted and believed him on his word, although everyone advised me to make it legal and have him a sign a contract. I refused to listen.

I was paying rent every month and I never asked for any money to operate the restaurant. I was doing so well that I ended up buying a house in Troy. I was the first Chaldean to purchase their own home in Troy city.

Don't Be Surprised that Life is Full of Surprises

One day a guest walked in and asked the server if he could speak with me. During our conversation, he said he wanted me to do business with his company, supplying all of his stores—the delis and the grab-and-go departments. I started providing what he wanted and all of a sudden, I was receiving calls from several different retailers to supply them.

The restaurant was bustling and now this wholesale business also took off. I was the first producer of hummus and pita chips with flavors in the country and the only one supplying retail stores. I was on the cover of *Michigan Hospitality* magazine! There were three pages inside the magazine about me. The restaurant became so popular that you had to make a reservation before coming. We were so busy that I had to ask Sheri to come and help me with hosting. She worked five days a week while my mother-in-law was taking care of the children.

Well, I've never met an entrepreneur who didn't have stories about hard-won lessons, and I was about to learn one early in my experience as a business owner. In fact, I learned that at that time, I was not a business owner after all. I had been misled, to put it mildly. The restaurant was in a shopping center and my cousin owned the plaza. The chef and his wife had a written agreement to run the restaurant with 50% ownership and pay rent to occupy the space—but the restaurant was operating for several years and my cousin never received any rent from the restaurant part of the plaza. Since he never received rent from his chef/partner, when the partnership broke up, they took each other to court.

Then my cousin hired a manager that didn't work out. He never told me about the partnership and legal proceedings with the chef. The business was in a mess in every way when I was asked to come to the rescue. The challenge and the opportunity for ownership appealed to me, but I was blind-sided because I assumed it was okay to pour all of my efforts, innovations, and hard work into a paper-thin container: A legally-binding written contract is the solid foundation one needs for a serious business, period.

How did I discover this fatal flaw? The staff started telling me things about the restaurant's history. I asked my cousin to have a meeting regarding our partnership, but he refused. I later learned it was because he and his wife were planning to get rid of me as the restaurant operator. Early one morning, his wife and his CPA came to the restaurant to tell me the bad news that I was no longer associated with the restaurant. I collected all of my belongings and left. I asked the CPA if my cousin was aware of this, and the CPA's response was that yes, it was his decision. When I came home, Sheri was there, thank goodness. She was very supportive and helped me quickly get over my shock.

I decided to wait until 3 p.m. and see if my cousin would call and say why he did that to my family and me. He didn't call. So, I called all the wholesale customer accounts and told them that I was no longer associated with the restaurant. They wanted me to personally supply them with what they needed, and I agreed.

One by one, they called the restaurant to cancel all their orders. After about fifteen minutes, my cousin called and threatened me. He was insulting my family in dirty and ugly language. He sued me for almost 100 thousand dollars, claiming that I stole from him. I knew I had done nothing wrong and figured I would have to go to court. After a few months, his wife was diagnosed with breast cancer. In our culture, to help heal the sick, we do our best to pray and practice forgiveness, so he dropped the case.

"We can't all be good at everything. This is partly the logic behind having a team in the first place...every job and every strength is covered."

—Simon Sinek

CHAPTER SEVEN

Always Have a Great Team

One of the customers I was supplying let me use his store kitchen until I could get on my feet and have my own place. With only my mother helping me, I worked to make and package the products and deliver them to all the stores. Before long, we had enough steady business to enable us to look for our own facilities and we soon found a great place to rent. It was a culinary school, which was big enough to grow my business.

My company started to develop rapidly, and we needed to hire more people. As the Choice to Own Your Power affirms, we each have unique talents, but we must be smart about recognizing what is not a strength and to be resourceful—i.e., bring others into the picture. Owning your power doesn't mean that you should have all the answers and feel all-powerful; instead, stand in the powerful position of knowing that every resource you require is out there, so get busy!

We had an urgent need for a refrigerated van to transport and deliver my perishable items. My friend in Sacramento loaned me $25K to purchase the van and my business took off. Apparently, I was doing so well that the landlord felt compelled to increase my rent, more than once, until it was four times what I had counted on. I took it as a nudge to make a change.

Being pushed to look for another location turned out to be a huge blessing. We took over a restaurant which was five minutes from my house.

This business was truly a team effort—a family team effort, in fact. My mother, Sheri, Rita (my sister), her husband, two cousins and I were operating the business. We had a restaurant in the front and my wholesale operation in the back. I started a great line of eight flavors of salad dressings and I began to travel and get involved in promoting the company at manufacturing food shows. My style of dressing was unique, all Mediterranean flavors; there was nothing like it anywhere.

I set up at the huge food manufacturing show in New Orleans. Many food distribution companies picked up my line, and I was lucky I found a food company that could manufacture and bottle my dressings and take care of the distribution. We had orders streaming in from all over the country! We continued our manufacturing and wholesale business with the other products.

I became good friends with the bottling company owner whom I met in New Orleans. He lived in Cincinnati, Ohio. I took a vacation with my family to Cincinnati and stayed with him and his family. On our first morning, he took us out on his yacht. He also showed me his manufacturing facility, which was huge. I came back home, even more optimistic about the salad dressing part of the business. My dressing was on the shelves in several different states. The surprise came about two weeks after returning from that trip.

My Cincinnati friend called me. There were widespread complaints coming into stores about my salad dressing. Tragically, all eight flavors had been contaminated during the manufacturing or bottling process. Bacteria caused the product to go bad. Upset customers demanded refunds and the stores removed all the inventory from their shelves. Thousands of dollars were lost.

The man who had hosted us at his home was a lovely guy, and I didn't sue him. Although I lost that business, I let it go…but I learned a lot. And, our friendship endures to this day.

Another Adventure

We built a thriving restaurant at our location and customers came back so often that they started to know me and many of my family members. One of the customers happened to be my neighbor and she was a professor at Michigan State University. One day she was in my restaurant having lunch with the Vice President of Domino's Pizza. He complimented my wife on the food and service-with-a-smile atmosphere and asked her if I could meet with him.

Remember the principles of hospitality I outlined in Chapter Five? This man was the VP of a multinational restaurant company and was able to instantly recognize what our establishment was all about. He wanted me to come to Domino's headquarters and speak in front of all his district managers. When I asked him what he wanted me to present to them, he told me to just be myself. And so I remind you, Choose to Be Yourself!

I went to Lansing, Michigan, to the district managers' conference and spoke on the topic of hospitality. As I wrote earlier in Chapter Five, I have natural abilities in this area plus workplace experience ever since I was a child helping my dad. When one chooses to embrace their own talents and power and then applies their strengths in the real world, they always "get lucky" like I did. Remember, luck is simply when preparedness meet opportunity. I was prepared, Domino's gave me an opportunity, and the outcome was fantastic. I had a great time, they loved my presentation and many stories to make each point, and I got paid very well. They asked me to come back many times!

Simply for speaking enthusiastically about how to treat people well, I felt rewarded and satisfied in many ways. It's a wonderful feeling when you Choose to Help Others Feel Alive and Connected—the essence of hospitality!

"A happy family is but an earlier heaven."

—George Bernard Shaw

Ashley, Dylan, Derek, me, and Sheri (2000)

Family

My favorite part of the day at our restaurant was when my very young children were coming hungry to the restaurant with their soccer cleats all muddy—they went straight to the kitchen and made themselves sandwiches. Customers loved my kids. After we closed the doors at the end of the day, my mother would go over to my sister's to babysit for an hour.

One night, my brother-in-law called to tell me that my mother was in the hospital and that he was coming to pick me up. I anxiously waited as near as possible to her hospital room, stopping three different doctors who walked by to ask them about my mother. One doctor informed me that my mother had died. It was very tough for me. I had lived with my mother most all of my life. *Rest in peace, my beautiful mom.*

*My mother-in-law Claire Hogan, father-in-law Earnest Hogan,
and my mother Siham*

One of my customers noticed that I was doing very well in my business and asked me if I needed an investor. It felt like it was indeed time to expand. He became a partner only in the wholesale part of the company and we ended up buying the building which I was renting. I started facing all types of competition and companies were giving out their product so cheap, just to get me out of business. That's exactly what happened. The partnership didn't go well, and we closed the business.

I started getting very tired and burned out, so I decided to sell the company and the house and move to Arizona. Sheri agreed. Why Arizona? That area was developing like crazy, with opportunities and possibilities in every profession! And the housing was still very cheap!

We sold the restaurant and I went to Arizona to look for a home. I got a job as a server at an Italian restaurant while waiting for a call from Fairmont Scottsdale Princess Resort, since I applied there for the position of dining room manager. The next day when I woke up, I received a call from Sheri. She asked me to get home as soon as possible because she and her mom had been in a car accident. I went back and took care of both of them, full-time, for about four months.

I started to work at the Red Fox restaurant, which became very famous after Jimmy Hoffa was last seen there. When Dylan graduated from high school, he said he would like a trip to San Diego to see his cousins, as a graduation gift. I asked my sister if it was okay for Dylan to come and visit them. Of course, she opened the doors for him. After he was there only three days, he called me. "Dad, I love you, but I am not coming home. San Diego is heaven!"

He asked if I would ship his car to him, but it would be much less expensive for me to just drive it there myself. And I wanted to see this place that my son called "heaven." I too fell in love with the area, so I called Sheri and told her I was not coming back, either. I saw many opportunities in San Diego, and we started making plans to all move to nearby Chula Vista.

The Time I Almost Had a Bad Day

As we were getting ready to pack up and move, Sheri was diagnosed with an abdominal tumor. Our health insurance agency contacted us and recommended that we see a specialist for consultation. After the doctor concluded his medical examination of Sheri, he said to me, "I have good news and bad news, which one do you prefer to hear first?" I told him to tell me the bad news first. He said that to remove the tumor, they'd have to clear the entire area inside and that she would not be the same again. Then I asked what the good news was. He said that she would certainly survive the operation. After he said that, I almost killed him. He asked me why I had said I wanted to kill him. I told him just to give her a life with her eyes open to see her kids. I felt like I had been holding my breath for a long time, but finally had a thread of hope to hold onto.

The surgery was successful. Like so many things in life that could be devastating, it offered an opportunity to remember what is truly important in life. Despite all the things that happened to me, I didn't break down, and I continued to enjoy life with a great attitude. We later bought a house in Chula Vista, not too far from where my sister was living and where Dylan was going to college. Sheri recovered and we enjoyed our beautiful family more than ever.

"Success is not the key to happiness. Happiness is the key to success. If you love what you are doing, you will be successful."

—Albert Schweitzer

CHAPTER EIGHT

A Grand Plan and a Grand Am

I got a temporary job at Jonathan's Market in La Jolla as the deli department manager. It was a decent job, but I had my sights set on bigger plans. While working there, I asked all the vendors to help me find a kitchen location to rent. Luckily, one vendor found one for me. I gave my store manager two months' notice of my resignation before starting my own company. The owner of Jonathan's Market had no problem with that and we even agreed that he would be my first customer. He owned other locations as well, so I started supplying all his other stores.

I soon added other customers and the business was flourishing. People were very excited about my salads, pita chips, hummuses, and their health benefits.

A new orchard market was opening in Ramona, California. I visited the store and spoke to the deli manager. After the discussion, he placed an order for me to supply the entire deli case and the grab-and-go department. Honestly, I was both astonished and thrilled.

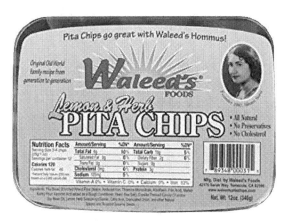

The demand was colossal. I went to three different wholesalers to purchase my commodities to get a better price. The kitchen I rented was small, located in a massive structure called "the flower building" where thousands of flowers were sold wholesale each day to flower shop owners. The kitchen was in a Mexican restaurant and there were more independent business people like me renting use of it. My leased time was from 4 p.m. to 12 midnight, which was perfect. I picked up Dylan and we started preparing the food for the new store and organized everything else.

We worked until 3 a.m., then we took a big chance by delivering the food items without having a proper truck. Sheri's personal effects in her car, a sporty Grand Am, were removed so that the products could be packed into the car. It was not easy setting things up, especially when I was the one to drive and the car seat was very low. I could barely see through the front windshield to move. However, we made it to the customer's store, but we had another challenge on our hands.

We didn't want the security guard to see us driving up in the Grand Am. We had to wait until he went around to the back of the building. Then we jumped out, grabbing shopping carts to load with all the products from the car and maneuvered them over to the front entrance. We were aware that the deli manager would be arriving soon (at 5 a.m.) and he came precisely at that time. We carted everything inside and stocked the products where they were supposed to be displayed.

Dylan and I sped off in the Grand Am to get home for a pit stop: to shower, change our clothes, and head back to our customer's store. We wanted to be there to introduce and explain all the new products to the employees as they arrived. Dylan and I didn't sleep. When the store opened, shoppers started streaming in. We showed them samples of our food, and people were ecstatic about it, especially the pita chips and flavored hummus. Within a few hours, half of the items were sold, which meant I had to get busy making more products for the next day! Then something happened that changed everything.

Going Global

I couldn't believe it when a broker representing Costco approached me to find out if I was interested in doing business with Costco. I could not say YES fast enough! He told me that he would let me know the date and time to bring my products and meet with Costco directors. We shook hands.

Costco, as you probably know, is an American company with discount stores referred to as wholesale clubs, in which bulk quantities of merchandise are sold at very discounted prices to club members who pay an annual membership fee.

It wasn't long after my family immigrated to the US that I learned about Costco from the consumer's point of view. I had never seen anything like it and was stunned at the abundance of quality foods and other items offered at affordable prices.

Costco customers are incredibly loyal. The company has over 100 million members as of this writing. Of those millions of members, over ninety percent renew their memberships. Its mission (see https://www.costco.com) is "to continually provide our members with quality goods and services at the lowest possible prices."

As an enthusiastic Costco shopper back in Michigan, I never in my wildest dreams thought I would one day be welcomed into Costco in California as a business partner, a vendor who provided their stores with products for their members to buy.

In order to achieve their mission, Costco conducts its business with the following Code of Ethics: Obey the law; Take care of our members; Take care of our employees; Respect our suppliers/vendors.

I found Costco to be a trustworthy partner who made me feel that they would support my business to grow and would care about having a sustainable long-term partnership. I always felt that my fundamental core values were aligned with Costco and its representatives who were my points of contact. They are often cited as one of the world's most ethical companies.

Back to when it all started...I received a phone call from the broker asking me to meet with buyers from Costco, one of the leading wholesale business operators in the world. It was real. I was not dreaming. At the meeting, I met two of the buyers and we hit it off. I had twenty items with me as samples that day, and I showed them eight different flavors of hummus, seven other salads, and five pita chips. At that time, there were no pita chips anywhere else in the country. I was the originator of offering America pita chips. The buyers tried the samples and they loved the flavors and quality. They asked everyone else in the building to come and taste to give their opinions. Every single taste-tester gave the products a thumbs-up.

The thing was, would customers buy these new products even if they did not get to try them first? In those days, people had no idea what *hummus* was. The buyers told me that at their store, there was a very limited selection of hummus—one vendor had two hummus flavors packaged in a 16-ounce container. The buyers were excited and wanted to bring my products to Costco, but they were doubting it would work. There was no way they could devote shelf space to my twenty-eight items.

I was not deterred! I knew I would just need to come back to them with a solution. The wheels in my mind started spinning and soon I was ready to meet again, this time with even more buyers in the room, and make my pitch.

When you Choose to Own Your Own Power, you proceed with an INTENTION to do your best with what you *do* have control over, and detach from everything outside of your control (so you don't waste your power with unproductive thoughts or worries). To do my best in this opportunistic event, I knew I must appear prepared, confident, and professional.

I wore my best suit. I carried a briefcase. This was my big opportunity to pitch Costco on my new original concept and get my food products into their stores.

The other suits in the room asked me a lot of questions. They also explained how their vendor agreements worked. As they spoke, I took notes on my notepad, using my very professional-looking pen.

Then I offered my ideas, something completely new. I persuaded Costco to sell my products on a consignment basis. They loved my idea! What they didn't know was that my briefcase was empty, I could not read or write English, and my entire food manufacturing business was just my son and me.

My concept was called the roadshow. I set up a table with free samples and products, staying in one location for five days. Costco's quota was for $250 in sales each day. On my first day, I sold half of my products by one o'clock in the afternoon. My sales were over eighteen hundred dollars!

They were so happy they started adding more stores every week. We ended up supplying all of California with 6.8 million dollars in revenue.

There is only one secret to my Costco success—my choice to act on my belief that I had a good idea and my confidence in myself to make it work.

What is sad to me is that so many people don't choose to act, they let fear stop them. They carry a briefcase full of fear around which is so limiting, when they could choose to be absent of fear, instead.

The Costco buyers and I reached an agreement for me to work with them on a consignment basis, with the condition that their boss needed to approve the plan. We all agreed that when they talked with him, they would bring along plenty of samples to help close the deal! They told me to expect a phone call from them.

I knew the market—it was the beginning of the health food craze. More and more people were interested in eating healthy products, and my products were all healthy and preservative-free. It was an ideal situation for me because demand was close to being greater than supply.

Dylan and I kept busy shopping, preparing, and delivering to our current accounts. Then I received a phone call from Costco telling me my starting day! They asked for the bar code and also specified that I must have each product labeled and the salads and hummus kept cold at each step. At that time, I had no refrigerated truck—no problem, I would rent one.

I went to my local print shop to order my labels. Then, we had to peel off each of the stickers to paste them on the containers. The workload was now getting to be too much. The company was growing and the amount of time that Dylan had to help me was limited due to his college schedule. I asked the person I rented the kitchen from if she knew anyone looking for a job. With her help, I employed two non-English-speaking women to join the company.

Very short on sleep, I somehow still had a lot of energy and enthusiasm to get everything ready for the big day, my first entry into the huge international company, Costco. The only truck I could find to rent for the delivery was a twenty-four-foot truck with a manual gear stick shift. That's a large truck, especially for someone who has very little experience driving any truck, much less a stick shift! However, it was great; I made it to Costco. It was 5 a.m. They checked everything, and I passed. They showed me my location and as I started setting up, the Costco staff was so kind in helping me.

It was like a dream; I was doing business with the biggest wholesaler in the world, standing right there in their store. After I got everything set up, I went to a restaurant nearby to refuel with a quick breakfast. I made a pit stop at home to shower and shave, but still no time for sleep. I went back to be there when the store opened.

Wow! I got very busy very fast. The customers of Costco thought that heaven had sent them an angel to teach them that eating could be both enjoyable and healthy. One out of every 10-12 shoppers bought my 3-item special. At one o'clock, half of all my product had been sold! Some buyers came to the booth asking if I had additional kinds of products. This never felt like work to me. Since I live choosing to help others feel alive and connected, every encounter was an energy boost, not an energy drain. The shoppers and the store employees were constantly engaging me. We had lots of laughs and fun together. At two o'clock, Dylan took over for me. I had to go shopping and get ready for the next day's supply.

Later that day, I received a phone call from Dylan that all the products were sold out! I got a call from one of the buyers pretend-scolding me because they had told me I needed to always keep my products stocked—they were actually very happy and excited. This was working out even better than either of us had expected.

I doubled the stock and increased my production capacity by asking my landlord to help get me two more employees. I was fortunate that one of the first employees was outstanding and I made her the supervisor. She really became my right hand and I gave her the recipes. She asked me if she could bring her son to work and help out, and I welcomed him in to join us. Now the only thing Dylan and I were doing was roadshows with Costco. I didn't have proper sleep for four months because I did not want to lose any of this opportunity.

The Costco roadshow started at Pacific Beach, which was our first location not far from their headquarters. This roadshow took on a new dimension different from Costco's former roadshows because no products had been sold before under a consignment agreement. My company started the concept. We started with five days a week in each location and traveled every week to a new place throughout the San Diego district. We were the revolutionary purveyors of hummus and pita chips in this country. We were introducing it to thousands every day, and people loved it.

The second location was Mission Valley, a stone's throw from Costco headquarters in Seattle, Washington. The news got to the main office and they sent their marketing department to check out the concept and the setup. They came to the booth, asking me all kinds of questions. They were shocked to see how many people were coming to the booth for tasting and buying. They congratulated me on the idea and the success. The roadshow was covered by the San Diego Tribune newspaper and they quoted Jim Sinegal, Costco founder, as saying how happy he was helping small companies like mine to grow.

It was 2002 and sales were growing by leaps and bounds. I heard that the Costco customers who bought the products from the first location, Pacific Beach, were asking Costco employees for Waleed's pita chips and hummus. They were told that we had been there for the show but had moved on to the next location. The buyers were not happy because they wanted my pita chips and hummus to remain in the store as products they could purchase any time. So, the Pacific Beach customers were driving down to Mission Valley to buy from me, saying that my products were fantastic and worth the travel distance! Some bought large quantities so that they didn't run out of stock quickly. I had never seen anything like this in my entire life.

The customers were helping us spread the word. As our product brand name became more and more known everywhere in California, every competitor now wanted to do the same concept at Costco. Every restaurant that carried pita bread was now selling pita chips. I never paid much attention to someone stealing my idea; I was only paying attention to how many thousands of people I made happy—if copying me was helping other businesses, that was fine with me. When asked, I was happy to share my thoughts with everyone.

We completed the roadshow in the San Diego district. My family and I headed out to do the roadshow at the Carlsbad location—my mother-in-law, Sheri, Dylan, Derek, Ashley, and me. It was Christmas Eve and I got very emotional. I was crying like a baby. I was overjoyed as I looked at my beautiful family, all of us pulling together and making a terrific success from our efforts. I also felt relieved and validated because Sheri had not wanted to come to California. She thought that we would not survive because California is known for its high cost of living. Our children were our priority, and all three were very active in their sports. At the time, I hugged her and told her that God would open doors for us. Seeing our children behind the tables interacting with the customers and Costco employees made us feel that we were expanding our sense of family all the time. It brought so much joy and happiness to me, though I was still going for days with almost no sleep at all.

I received a phone call from the buyers asking me to meet with them. They asked me to start doing two stores simultaneously—I had no problem with that! I accepted their conditions that I had to change my labels and add the nutritional information. I made all the changes and before they gave me the schedule, I asked for a favor—they said yes, I could take a ten-day break. Thank God!

I took Sheri on vacation and it was wonderful to spend time together, just the love of my life and me. We were on a yacht for several days, but I admit I slept most of the time. It was just what we both needed and we returned rested and refreshed.

We started the two-store shows and I was getting swamped. My landlord asked me to look for another location, that the place was way too small to accommodate the quantities of products we were producing, and that storage was not big enough to store everything in the restaurant. She was right. I searched for a larger space and found a banquet hall and restaurant that I transformed into a food manufacturing facility. Before I started up, Costco sent their team in charge of business operations over to do a full inspection of the place; we passed the test and started production.

I was overwhelmed with a barrage of paperwork and emails. At the start, all the paperwork was done by Dylan, but when my uncle heard how busy we were, he came and helped for two months until I hired someone to take care of the office administration and part of the marketing. When I was supplying the orchard market in Ramona, the deli manager and I became close friends. I got in touch with him and I found out that he was no longer with the orchard market. I approached him with the position and he accepted the offer. My uncle left and my friend was working with me, which was great.

From two stores every week to four stores every week, our company was getting bigger and bigger. The news about our products spread to the Los Angeles district and they already knew how well we were doing. They invited us in and we started with two stores and ended up with four at a time. The space the company was occupying was getting too small and we found another location, perfect to use for perishable items like hummus and salads.

Now, my friend was marketing the products all over the country and Costco started ordering truckloads of pita chips and some hummus to go to Arizona. They also ordered entire pallets of hummus for the San Diego district. I was fortunate to have good help. With all this happening, I still had time for Ashley's soccer.

Waleed's Foods company revolutionized the business in the United States, if not the world.

The pita chip product labels stated:

"The original Pita Chip, created by the Southern Californian chef, Waleed Soro. The perfect treat by themselves or for dipping. Strong, delicious and wonderfully addictive."

"When something is important enough, you do it even if the odds are not in your favor."

—Elon Musk

CHAPTER NINE

Choose to Love Yourself by Knowing What's Most Important

The business had become a beast, but I had no complaints. Thank goodness I had a wonderful family that I loved—this kept me from being gobbled up by the beast. Ashley was playing soccer at the highest level for her age group, competing as one of the best players in the country. I never missed her practices or games. Sheri and I both put Ashley's soccer as our priority. The best years of my life were those watching my baby's soccer! I would make some risky decisions so that I did not miss out on any of her activities. I was very fortunate to have the right people and operations in place in the company.

We had perfected the way we exhibited at food manufacturing shows and participated in these worldwide. We hoped to expand by being picked up by giants in addition to Costco, and we were successful in that goal. Every major wholesaler started carrying our pita chips: Walmart, Sam's Club, and more. We were in stores all over the country! We continued to do Costco roadshows in northern California, Arizona, Los Angeles, and Texas. Competitors, especially for the pita chips, all came into existence after the fact that I started the concept.

One competing company was bought out for millions because of my innovations they had taken advantage of and, believe me, the giants knew where the successful products originated. The same company that bought the competition came to me first! And I refused to sell. I wanted to stay Mom-and-Pop. This meant that I did not have the capacity to mass produce pita chips, even though Costco would have distributed them all over the country. Again, my choice was made after considering what was *most* important.

I discussed the proposition with my accountant, attorney, and of course my family. Selling would mean relinquishing 80% of the company…but 100% of my freedom. Given the choice, I did not want to be an employee of the company and perhaps miss important family time and especially Ashley's soccer games.

I don't regret the decision I made, because today I have things in my life that are more valuable to me—and thanks to God I am still enjoying the family with additions of daughter-in-law Nikki, my granddaughter Saige, grandson Zander, and my daughter-in-law Tyler!

How You Spend Your Time is How You Spend Your Life

When you choose to own your own power, you will have some tough decisions to make, as does everyone, but you'll have a firm place to stand as you decide on your next step.

Once you set out in the direction you choose, never forget that you are the one who took that turn. That means that it is up to you to make the most of it! With my renewed commitment to spend my time aligned with my priorities and values, I made doubly sure that I had my company and staffing set up to not just survive, but to thrive in my absence. This is when you know you truly have a successful business, not just a self-employment position. While it is technically true that I could take off any time, being my own boss, I would not feel the total freedom to do that unless my responsibilities to the company, its customers, and employees were being fulfilled.

A local supermarket closed its doors and I scooped up several out-of-work managers and employees. This meant that all of my bases were covered. I met with the department directors and showed them the sales revenues. I told them my expectation was that these revenues would not decrease, and, that if they increased, there would be profit sharing for all of the department directors. With this incentive in place, I felt especially confident that even as I was on the road with my daughter, all would be well in my company.

When you choose to own your own power, it doesn't mean you have to control everything and do everything yourself. It means that you know that you are powerful in being resourceful. You can figure out how to make things happen through your connections, resourcefulness, and leadership. With unwavering confidence in my staff and systems, I was as free as a bird to put my attention on where the family focus was at the time: Ashley's soccer.

Ashley was playing for one of the best clubs in the country. Some of the trainers were former national champions and her teammates and competing teams were all top-level players. Her life became soccer and more soccer. I shifted all of my attention to Ashley—that is, I was with her full time.

Of course, I kept in close contact with Dylan and others running the business. Hummus and pita chips were being sold everywhere in the country. Pita chips and hummus companies were opening doors and starting a business for themselves. All types of food establishments started to sell hummus and pita chips, from grocery stores to delis, and they became popular in restaurants, both casual and upscale. As consumers became more and more health food conscious, hummus skyrocketed in popularity as a healthier alternative to dips made with cheese and dairy fat.

Working long hours at food industry exhibition booths never bothered me, mainly because of the overwhelming number of people coming to the booth and saying how blessed they felt to have this food available! They could not stop praising this new healthy option that was full of freshness and flavor. They shared their smiles with me with every sample they took; you could see their happiness on their face, right there! And right there, that was my greatest reward. As I said, I choose to help others to feel alive and connected and so my desire was filled over and over with every visitor to the booth. It may be hard to believe, but I never thought about how much money these efforts would bring—I don't think I would have had as much fun if that was on my mind.

Embracing Change is Part of Just Being Yourself

As I've written earlier, everything has its time, its season. One thing that never changes is the fact that things always change. When you resist that, get angry about that, or try to ignore that, you will suffer. Then you can't enjoy just being yourself, can you? It's natural to be momentarily thrown off if there's a sudden change, but I promise you that you can train yourself to quickly respond instead of having a mood-crushing reaction. Respond by accepting that a change has occurred. Be aware of your thoughts and feelings, but the sooner that you embrace it as "what is," the sooner you can see what this new horizon might have to offer. Even when things are on a roll and all seems like roses and rainbows, keep your eyes and mind open to change. By looking at signs that forecast a change in the industry, I was able to prepare myself and be confident I would respond as well as possible.

And changes did occur. We were facing more and more competition, including one large company cutting prices in half, attempting to completely take over the market and put smaller companies like mine out of business.

With sales leveling off, I knew it was time to downsize and we gave up two buildings in order to lease one facility of just the right size. I also began to have more time for the business as Ashley's soccer career changed from travel teams to playing at the college level. In fact, she was granted a full scholarship to one of the top-ranked colleges in California, Saint Mary's in Moraga. That $200K was my gift from Ashley!

With my family's help, we kept the business going for two more years until 2009, when real estate and other major economic problems devastated so many companies and individuals. I had many investments in Arizona that I lost. Also, I lost my house in San Diego for a short sale! I took my family and moved to the wine country, found a small building suitable for making my product, then gave it to Ashley to run it. I opened a Mediterranean restaurant in Old Town Temecula and bought a house not far from there.

My son Dylan decided to pursue a career in Culinary Arts. He was accepted into the Culinary Institute of America in New York City. My family's work ethic is amazing—the epitome of teamwork. Between us, we operated the manufacturing business and the restaurant for twelve years. We made a decision to close the food products business as the business climate turned unfavorable with rising operating costs and an explosion of competition. Chef Dylan began to run the restaurant, expanding into other markets and opening additional locations.

My children feel completely free (as they should) to pursue their own interests and use their own unique gifts. Ashley is enjoying success as a fitness model and personal coach and trainer. She is quite unique in her approach to fitness, having her clients start with self-reflection and inner work, which makes their efforts to change their diet and exercise habits much easier to achieve. Rather than a focus on goals for looking a certain way, her clients achieve life-changing progress, healing and improving from the inside out.

In the next section, Part Three, you will find very specific ways that you can make this book practical and valuable to you as a daily tool. Included there is a wonderful contribution from Ashley. As an example of a young adult who is utilizing The 5 Cornerstone Choices, her perspective and words of encouragement are just what I want for you to take to heart.

Ashley Soro, International WBFF (World Beauty Fitness and Fashion) Competition in Las Vegas, Nevada (2021)

With similar passions, her brother Derek leads fitness programs for people all over the country and has built a stellar reputation in that field. Recently, God blessed us with a new member of the family, Taylor. I pay her the highest compliment by saying that she is another Sheri. She is a sweet daughter-in-law and I am proud to call her my daughter.

Derek and his wife, Taylor

Dylan started to operate the restaurant, and he is doing great. He started another company within the restaurant and just opened a second location! The whole family helps out with the operation. For Sheri and I, we love our "job" when we get to babysit our grandkids. We have a dear daughter-in-law, Nikki, a beautiful human being. I have no idea how she does it! Dylan is a fortunate man for having Nikki in his life; she is an occupational therapist, she operates the administration for the restaurants, and is a great mom to their two kids. I am proud to call her my daughter.

Zander, Nikki, Dylan, and Saige

Currently, I am devoting my free time to reading, writing, and speaking to audiences. In the fall of 2022, in fact, I will be giving a TEDx talk! I am planning to write my next book about the hospitality industry.

First communion for my great-nephews Ralph, Rocky, and Roman Daoud

Family celebrating my great-nephew Roman's christening

Sophia and Elena Soro, my great- nieces

Santanah Daoud,
my great-niece

Maximus Wallace,
my great- nephew

From top left, my brothers Bill, Tom, and me; bottom left, my sisters Kelly,
Rita, and Basima

George Daoud, my nephew
He was only 31 years old when he passed away on October 28, 2020.

The strength of our family bond is immeasurable—we're a team. As individuals, I see the threads of commonality, namely the core values of integrity and love. The Five Choices were never posted on the wall as a creed to live by, but each of us has countless stories where choosing to love yourself, or choosing to help others to feel alive and connected, or any of the crucial choices I've distinguished for you in this book have made and continue to make life incredibly rich.

Here is a simple truth worth thinking about until you know it in your bones: When you have one good day after another, you **are** building your whole, best, rewarding life.

Now is the time to heighten your awareness of all the daily choices you make. Use the wisdom found in The 5 Cornerstone Choices. With this awareness, you can make choices that will lead to an incredibly rich and rewarding life no matter your circumstances. And when you do, you too can join me in saying, "I've never had a bad day."

Next, PART THREE is for you to not only read, but to **use**. Perhaps you feel motivated to grab the steering wheel of your life right now, but *staying* motivated is an entirely different thing. PART THREE provides you with resources, exercises, and *actions*—because, it is crucial to remember that MOTIVATION FOLLOWS ACTION (not the other way around!).

PART THREE

"Action is the foundational key to all success."

—Pablo Picasso

Actions, Exercises, and Resources to Facilitate Change

> "God grant me the serenity to accept the things I cannot change, the courage to change the things I can, and the wisdom to know the difference."
>
> —Reinhold Niebuhr

This book's purpose is to persuade you to change your thoughts and actions so that you are living your best life every day...by letting go of fear and living by these principles I call THE 5 CORNERSTONE CHOICES.

1. **Choose to Love Yourself**

2. **Choose to Be Yourself**

3. **Choose to Own Your Own Power**

4. **Choose to Help Others to Feel Alive and Connected**

5. **Choose to Never Have a Bad Day**

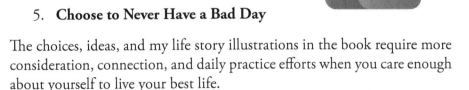

The choices, ideas, and my life story illustrations in the book require more consideration, connection, and daily practice efforts when you care enough about yourself to live your best life.

Exercises to Empower Your Cornerstone Choices

Here are some actions to take, deeper points to consider, and resources to check out in order to discover more of what you as an individual need for support. Everyone is different, but please know there are resources and connections that are perfectly matched to empower you.

1 INSPIRATION AND INTENTION

Let's start with an inspirational message. Ashley Soro, my daughter who is important to the narrative of the book, contributes the following—a personal note from her to you:

Choosing to Love Yourself Starts with Good Health and Self-Compassion

–Ashley Soro–

Being a certified personal trainer and online fitness and nutrition coach, I have so many clients who realize the obvious changes that are going to take place once they start working with me.

They know they're going to have to plan exercise into their schedule. They're going to have to change the way they eat. They're probably going to do their best to get more sleep, drink more water, and take their vitamins.

Yes, they may even go as far as implementing a full-on morning routine (I even try to rebel against this one because as much as I feel amazing with structure, my brain loves chaos instead, so the monotony of a routine makes me want to do the opposite.)

They know how important mindset work is. They may implement journaling, meditating, and/or going for walks to free up space in their minds.

But are they going to do any of those things (and continue to do those things) if they lack self-compassion? Probably not. You may ask, why do I say that?

Because the reason we stop doing them consistently is usually because we've decided in our own minds that we are either 1) incapable 2) lack discipline 3) are just not motivated enough or 4) _____ (insert all of the nasty things you say to yourself on a daily basis).

The reason I know this is so prevalent and so important to talk about is because my level of self-compassion was at an all-time low during a period in my life when I was very unsure of what I truly wanted.

Any missed training session, poor eating decision, and/or failure in really any aspect of my life put me in a downward spiral of "I suck, I'm never going to accomplish what I want to accomplish, I'm letting everyone down, people have it way worse than me, I'm pathetic..." the list goes on.

This is exactly when we have to VALUE being compassionate towards ourselves, even if we don't feel like we deserve it.

So, when you're really not feeling like being kind to yourself, are you able to have an INTENTION to be compassionate towards yourself?

I'm willing to bet that if you implored just a bit more self-compassion, you'd be that less likely to throw in the towel when life happens and you neglect exercise, eat an extra cookie, or maybe even gain a pound back.

Maybe that makes one less time you stop and start yet another program!

But if we've never actually been self-compassionate... how do we start?

The first step I have most of my clients take, especially if they've always struggled with self-compassion, is to imagine they were having a conversation with their daughter.

Even if they have yet to have children, hypothetically, they wouldn't dare say the nasty things they say to themselves to a small child. So why not imagine you were talking to that small child?

Once you can imagine having that conversation, you can then imagine that little child is a younger version of yourself. Once again, would you put yourself down the way you do now? I'd like to think that you would be quite a bit more lenient on the younger, more impressionable version of yourself.

The second step is to become more self-aware in the moments you begin to slip into that downward spiral of negativity.

If you're sitting here asking yourself, am I self-aware? Or, how do I become more self-aware? There are different ways you can explore this, but I will give you a few to get you started.

If you're able to recognize your emotions while you're feeling them, and understand why you're feeling them, you're probably more self-aware than you think. You may not always respond and/or react the way you'd prefer to, but even just understanding the emotions is a step in the right direction.

If you find yourself constantly searching for more perspective, more knowledge, more understanding, and recognize that there really is so much that you don't actually know, you're practicing self-awareness. It's a beautiful thing to accept that we will always be learning; without growth, what is life?

Diving deeper into that, if you're able to understand other perspectives and opinions and are able to accept them even if you disagree, you're really getting the gist of this whole self-awareness thing.

It's a beautiful thing to connect with individuals who have a completely different thought process and see the world in an entirely different lens; the more we step into this understanding, the more we grow individually as well.

The beauty of perspective also gives you freedom in the moments you blame yourself for another person's emotions or inability to understand you. If you struggle with self-compassion, you are far more likely to see yourself as the issue in moments like these.

There are so many benefits to practicing more self-awareness, but in the journey to finding more compassion for yourself, it is crucial.

All of that being said, I also want to give you some tips on how you can implement small changes into your life that, with the added tips on implementing more self-compassion, will push you even further ahead in this journey of yours. Remember, small changes, because the simpler we make this process, the more likely we are to find success!

Because we love the number "5" in the Soro family, here are "5 Steps to a More Positive and Purposeful Life."

STEP 1: Add 3 walks each week

Notice how I didn't say walk 30 minutes every single day (at least when you're first starting out and think a walk is from your room to the couch to watch Netflix.) If you don't have an issue walking 30 minutes every single day already, by all means, keep that in your regimen. It's great for you. If you're someone who falls off completely and just needs to implement something in order to feel accomplished, start small and work your way up.

STEP 2: Don't commit to 5 workout days

Are you catching my drift here? Commit to less workout days so you can add to your schedule vs. take away. The taking away will only make you feel like you're "incapable" and you are far from that! We are so quick to tear ourselves down when we are not perfect and that's precisely why we start and stop so many different programs, even when we know we truly want it! This is also why I disagree when someone says, well, you just didn't want it enough. Why do I disagree with that? Because I knew how badly I wanted to accomplish certain goals, but I didn't realize that I was taking on too much in order to do just that. So, remember, start small! Add in 2 days of exercise, then work up to 3, and if at that point you're feeling on top of the world, move to 4!

STEP 3: Add one self-love habit each month

Once again, I am a firm believer in **less is more**. Imagine if you nailed that self-love habit CONSISTENTLY for the entire month (instead of adding three and only doing these for a week, and then that nasty cycle comes rearing its ugly head back into the equation). This is when we implement some good ol' perspective! **One self-love habit practiced consistently for the month is better than a dozen tried and abandoned.**

STEP 4: Create a 3-5 step morning or nightly routine (keep this VERY basic)

I can't even begin to explain how many times I have attempted to nail a 10-step daily routine in the morning and evening. I would do all of it for a few days or I would only finish parts of it, and then I'd go weeks without doing anything at all. Then the negative self-talk would get LOUD. And here we are starting back over again. We have to give ourselves tasks that we can accomplish! The act of accomplishment is what ultimately gives us the belief in ourselves that we really CAN do this!

STEP 5: Limit your caffeine intake and don't consume it past 4 p.m.

Ok, so this goes for all of my coffee lovers. I knew how bad my dependence on caffeine was, but I really didn't understand it until I cut back (I'm talking 200-300 mg less each day) and started getting the most rested sleep of my life and actually woke up refreshed! The concept of sleeping and not waking up tired was foreign to me, even with 7-8 hours! Quality of sleep here is important, and caffeine will absolutely affect that.

Alright so, these changes don't seem drastic, right?! They were massive within my own life. The truth is that I have tried and failed to be consistent with many things in my life, so many times, and I know what works and what doesn't.

We create this narrative in our own minds that we're just made to fail. In those moments when we attempt to accomplish it all at once, whether or not it was a burst of creative energy or a fleeting moment of motivation, we have to remind ourselves of our vicious cycles and push ourselves to remain consistent.

Consistency is our issue—and when we're feeling down in the dumps, consistency with the things that you know you have to do (which are also the things you absolutely do not want to do) are what pulls you out of that negative bubble.

I hope at the end of this you're able to implement some of these habits within your own routine, and I hope you know that you are not alone in this process as we are all trying to live a more purpose driven and positive life.

Follow Ashley on Instagram: ashleysorolifestyleandfitness

and visit her website: www.ashleysoro.com.

More Exercises to Empower Your Cornerstone Choices

2 KNOWING YOURSELF

You may think you know yourself already, but there are actually an infinite number of layers to each individual—that's what makes people so uniquely interesting. Here are 12 questions to spend some time with. Think about each one, not only right now, but again after one month, and in six months, or every year on your birthday. If you keep a written journal for this exercise, you will be fascinated to discover what changes and what stays the same, over time.

As you work on this exercise, you must remember this one thing: Be honest! This is just for you. You don't have to ever share it with anyone unless you really want to. There are no "right" or "wrong" answers. Just make note of what's there during your self-inquiry.

Questions to help you know yourself better:

1. Who matters most to me? Who are my support people?

2. What do I like to do for fun?

3. What new activities am I interested in or willing to try?

4. What are my strengths?

5. What are my values? What do I believe in?

6. What do I keep as secret out of shame or worry about others' opinions?

7. Where do I feel safest? With whom?

8. If I could erase my fear, I would _____.

9. What do I most love talking about with others?

10. Do I have favorites? A book? Movie? Band? Food? Color? Animal?

11. My IDEAL job would be _____

12. What am I grateful for?

Often, it seems hard to answer even basic questions about yourself. Isn't that strange? At some point, you were conscious of all of these thoughts, beliefs, and feelings within you, even if only for a moment. This exercise helps you to remember who you are. RE-MEMBERING yourself is a journey into your true self (that's where you can connect with self-love).

ALSO: Come up with your own measures of "who I am and how I'm doing." The personal-to-you ones are the only measuring sticks of lasting importance in your life.

RE-MEMBERING yourself is a process. You don't need to rush through all these questions today! I suggest answering only one or two per day so you can explore them in-depth. But work at your own pace–perhaps one per week is more realistic for you.

3 FOCUS YOUR GROWTH

Forget Envying, Copy-catting or Feeling Inferior to Those You Put on a Pedestal

Here are two ways you can use your imagined "heroes" as a way to help you create your own unique voice and style, without being an imitator or discounting your true self:

1. Think of someone you deeply admire. Write a list of the things you like about them and get specific about why. Do the same for things you dislike. This gives you a practical overview of what attracts you,

or not—you don't need to try and BE someone else, just notice what you'd like to adopt from their attitudes, behaviors, and skills. It's okay to acknowledge that they are not perfect…no one is. Do this for all your heroes and idols.

2. Think of your differentiators. Of all the people you most admire, who are you most similar to? How are you alike and, importantly, how are you different? Choosing to be yourself means you know something about what makes you unique and you embrace and celebrate that.

 # CONNECTION WITH YOUR TRUE NATURE

1. Get in touch with your inner child.

If you ever watch small children, you will notice just how free they are and how little they care about what other people think of them. They are happy and in the moment. Or maybe they are not happy and are not about to fake it! They're just being present to their feelings and expressing them authentically.

They are their true natures. They have not yet been socialized to "fit in" to a society that squashes that. They don't care if people think that they are silly while they dance in the front yard for all of the neighbors to see.

Children are just pure love and light. If you really want to get in touch with your inner child, become freer. Play, have fun, enjoy the moment, do cartwheels in the front yard.

We play roles to fit into society and we suppress our true nature out of fear of what others think. If you find yourself worrying about being judged, remember that is merely just the socialized you, not the real you.

Action step: Go to a busy playground and observe children for 30 minutes. If you go with a friend and their kids to the park, that is fine, but to drink in the experience, you need to be quiet and not in conversation for as long as possible. Just observe the kids at play. Notice your thoughts about their energy, lack of fear, and especially notice what memoires and associations come up for you from your own childhood. Make a plan to find time in the coming week to go outside and play, whatever that looks like for you now. Choose something that is out of your "grown-up" comfort zone.

2. Become more aware of your thoughts.

> ### You are not your thoughts.

The ONLY things that get in the way of you being freely yourself are knotted thoughts and tangles of "shoulds," which encumber your freedom to be.

Consider this: stop believing that some of what you hear (the voice in your head) is really "you" and some of it is not. Obviously, if you hear the voice, you are the observer. "You" are not generating these automatic thoughts.

Allow yourself to sit quietly every morning before starting your day for five to ten minutes.

Just allow them to float in and circle around, without getting attached to them. Just observe them. When you are finished, continue observing the mind throughout your day.

You may be shocked by the number of negative or disempowering thoughts. After so long, our reality begins to take shape based on all of these conditioned thinking patterns.

We are all so much more than those old negative thinking patterns would ever allow us to believe.

How will this practice affect your ability to make the Choice to Be Yourself? Imagine that you show up for a play rehearsal where you've agreed to be an actor. The director is not there yet. You're eager to get into costume and begin learning your lines…but how do you know which character you are to play? Only when you know who you are—and are not—can you start being yourself!

Action step: Become more aware of the quality of your thinking. In the morning or any quiet time during the day, spend 3-5 minutes simply noticing your thoughts.

Yes, thoughts will come and go, but just allow them to do that without getting attached to them. Just observe them. When you are finished, continue observing the mind throughout your day.

We have so many unconscious beliefs that we have taken on over the years that were probably handed down to us from somebody else, and that we believed to be who we are. Becoming more aware of the quality of your thoughts, letting go of the old beliefs, and becoming more present can help in revealing your true nature.

We are all so much more than those old negative thinking patterns would ever allow us to believe.

Resource:

Those negative voices take on different personalities, which Shirzad Chamine calls "saboteurs." He developed a brilliant, short assessment you can take (for free) to discover your own saboteurs.

https://assessment.positiveintelligence.com/saboteur/overview

"Saboteurs are the voices in your head that generate negative emotions in the way you handle life's everyday challenges. They represent automated patterns in your mind for how to think, feel, and respond. They cause all of your stress, anxiety, self-doubt, frustration, restlessness, and unhappiness. They sabotage your performance, wellbeing, and relationships," writes Chamine.

Shirzad Chamine is the author of the New York Times bestselling *Positive Intelligence*. Shirzad has lectured on Positive Intelligence at Stanford University and has trained faculty at Stanford and Yale business schools.

Once you become aware of your own "saboteurs," how do you quickly get on and stay on a more positive track? You can learn to master your own "Positivity Quotient" (PQ) with the help of a coach, an app, and other resources. Teresa Bueno is a professional coach who uses PQ training techniques to help you use your mind to work for you, not against you.

Contact Teresa: PQMasterCoach@gmail.com.

 IDENTIFY YOUR STRENGTHS

Here are a few examples of what I mean by your "strengths." See if any of these describe you:

- Communication: It is natural for you to put your thoughts into words, whether spoken or written. You are a good conversationalist and enjoy sharing your ideas with others.

- Developing others: You see the potential in others more easily than others do and probably better than the person sees for himself. You get satisfaction from being a catalyst for others' personal or professional growth.

- Strong empathy: You feel more than sympathy or compassion, you feel what someone else is feeling. You can sense their feelings and imagine yourself in their situation.

- Enthusiasm: Others can feel your passion from a block away. Your positivity is contagious and you find that you effortlessly persuade others to become excited, too.

- Relationships: Connection is your middle name. You enjoy a variety of different types of people, finding a connection where others would not perceive one exists. Sometimes you are the essential glue holding a group together to work or play in a harmonious or constructive way.

Other strengths you may identify with include curiosity, perseverance, organization, or influencing. Think about what you have experienced time and again that worked for you when you tapped into something inside of yourself...

What do you think your strengths are?

What do you think others would say a strength of yours is that you did not mention?

Identify and build on your strengths. This will make living by The 5 Cornerstone Choices easier and the rewards deeply satisfying.

Resource:

There is an excellent and revealing assessment tool that has been used by thousands of individuals, teams, educators, and organizations which measures the intensity of your talents in each of the "34 Clifton Strengths" themes. These 34 themes represent what people do best. They categorize all that's right with humankind—distilled down to 34 different themes.

https://www.gallup.com/cliftonstrengths/en/253850/cliftonstrengths-for-individuals.aspx

Immediately after completing the Clifton Strengths assessment, you'll receive your results in a report featuring *customized* descriptions of your rank-ordered dominant strengths.

Completing the online talent assessment (formerly the Clifton Strengths Finder) is your way to:

- discover what you naturally do best

- learn how to develop your greatest talents into strengths

- use your personalized results and reports to maximize your potential

6 ACTION STEP TO NEVER HAVE A BAD DAY

Could there be a more crystal-clear way to live your life "never having a bad day" than by simply *choosing* to do so?

It is fruitless at best, tragic perhaps, to *wish* for such a positive, joy-filled life. "If only" *circumstances, friends, family, bosses, health reports, and the ambient temperature itself would just line up in the precise manner we imagine would suit us perfectly…*

No, that is not how life works.

Choose, first thing in the morning and all day long, to have a good day!

There is no power in all of the universe which can stop you from choosing, for yourself, to never have a bad day.

Choose.

7 SELF-GUIDED MEDITATION

Record your own voice using your phone, tablet, or PC and use these affirming words that I wrote for both you and me to use. I recommend starting your day with it AND having this guided meditation handy whenever you feel that peace is missing. A feeling of peace is the cloud your "having a good day" can float on.

Welcome to these positive words for inner peace, love, and happiness.

*   *   *   *   *

I let go of all that doesn't serve me to live my best life.

I choose to connect with a state of inner peace.

I choose to love myself.

I choose to be myself.

I choose to own my own power.

I choose to help others to feel alive and connected.

I choose to never have a bad day.

I allow myself to heal, I am healing, I am becoming calmer, my breath is slow and relaxed, I am connecting with the comforting silence of my soul.

I am aligned with my higher consciousness, I am connected to inner wisdom, I trust the flow of life, everything is occurring in the best way, things are happening for my greatest good.

I am blessed and protected, I am rising higher, my body is light, and my mind is calm, I am tuned to the frequency of love, I am in sync with the universe.

I am kind to myself, I accept myself for who I am, I acknowledge my strengths, I embrace my weaknesses, I am proud of who I am, I am proud of what I have accomplished, constantly my life improves, I love and respect myself.

I deserve peace and happiness, every breath I take fills me with ease.

I radiate peace and love to others, I am relaxed and welcome joy.

I live in the moment, my mind is at peace, I am where I am meant to be. In this moment, I welcome beautiful experiences into my life, I can overcome difficulties with ease, I am confident of my abilities to succeed.

I let go of things I can't control, I detach from people who don't add value to my life, I forgive people who've hurt me, I forgive myself, I choose peace.

I choose to love myself, I am deeply loved by myself and others, I am surrounded by people who support me to live my best life, I love life to the fullest, I see the brighter side of life, I know the brilliance of everything in my life.

I radiate positivity, I choose to never have a bad day, I'm grateful for all my blessings, I am thankful for all my life lessons, my life lessons are making me a better person, each lesson helps me to better live my best life, my life is getting better each day, life is beautiful, all is well.

All is well.

8 MINDFULLNESS EXERCISE

1. Sit, take an upright, relaxed posture, and practice mindfulness of breathing for a few minutes. Follow this with a period of "mindfulness of body" practice, opening awareness to body sensations as they arise.

2. Do you notice any unpleasant aspects of experience that are present at the moment? Are you feeling discomfort or pain anywhere in the body? If so, where? What about difficult emotions? If there are some, ask yourself where they are and which sensations appear. Be aware of any tightness, pressure, restlessness, heat, throbbing, and so on.

3. Bring attention gently to the thoughts in your mind. Are these pleasant or unpleasant? Notice any reactions to arising sensations or thoughts. Are you tending to pull away from them, get annoyed by them, ruminate on them, or are you reacting in some other way? Without buying into them or trying to stop them, simply notice these reactions with kindness and interest.

4. Now, turn your attention towards an unpleasant sensation, a region of intensity in the body. It could be a subtle sensation or more pronounced. With gentleness, direct the mind's eye to this area and tune into what you find. Allow yourself to feel whatever sensation is there, softly. You could imagine breathing into the sensation as you inhale, and breathing out from it as you exhale, letting it be experienced with the rhythm and flow of the breath. Without trying to change it in any way; just offer it a kind space in which to happen. See if you can let go of any attempt to eliminate it or distract from it. Just offer your curiosity, being with it, moment by moment. Is the sensation moving at all, shifting in location, intensity, or quality?

5. Notice any thoughts that arise concerning the feeling, and let these pass through in the background of awareness, without trying to follow or stop them. Let go of trying to think your way out of the

difficult experience. Just let it be, embracing it as compassionately as you can.

6. Bring your attention away from your thoughts and feelings and body sensations and only focus on your breath. Inhale slowly, exhale. Inhale slowly, exhale. Now put your consciousness in your body wherever it is touching a grounding surface like the floor or chair seat.

Move towards your next desired action for the day, feeling free and at peace.

9 CHOOSE TO HELP OTHERS TO FEEL ALIVE AND CONNECTED

1. Write down this 6-word note and post it where you will see it often. You can make several of these notes if you want to give yourself a more frequent reminder that:

Vitality Is A Function Of Participation

2. Make a list of things which prohibit your participation with "here and now." For example, if you are having lunch with a friend but you are looking at your phone. That's not participating in the present moment or the extraordinary opportunity to have an authentic, in-person connection with someone. Technology has a wonderful role to play in your life, but you must decide when it serves you. Nothing replaces human interaction.

You can identify things to list by noting what's missing that has you say "no" to participating. Maybe you were invited to go to the beach, but you don't have what you consider the "right swimsuit" or the "right swimsuit body" so you declined to participate.

Have you been meaning to call your favorite aunt but haven't made the time to do so? One item on your list might be "too busy." Bring to mind something creative or fun you've been wanting to do—join a bowling league, paint terra cotta planters to give as gifts, join the music team at church. What's stopping you? Write these on your list.

Look over your list and pick one next item to say YES to. Do that NOW.

Make it a goal to participate in something every day that would be easy to skip or put off until some other time. "There's no time like the present!"

Sometimes the most profound CHOICE starts with simply saying YES.

The second significant benefit to participating in life (in addition to vitality) is that you create opportunities for feeling "touched." This is one of the best feelings you can feel. Think of a time when someone said something or did something that touched your heart. It may have made you feel inspired, or very sad, or in awe...but the point is, it made you FEEL ALIVE. This is part of vitality, and it's how you feel connected with yourself, God, and others.

Without connection, life is cold and scary. You wouldn't wish that on others, right? So you get to make the choice to help others to feel alive and connected—in this effort, you also will feel more alive and connected.

- Today or very soon, when you are in a conversation, listen for and point out the talents, strengths, or gifts of the other person. What's unique? Acknowledge them for who they are instead of just complimenting them on what they've done.

- From your Choice to Love Yourself and to Be Yourself, you will be seen by others as genuine and self-secure—so much so that they, too, can feel secure. Others will be attracted to being around you as they feel increasingly safe and confident in themselves. Today, or very soon, use self-deprecating humor or a confession of your own weakness or mistake to lower the wall between you and another person. Notice if they step through the opening. Focus on being "interested" not "interesting."

- Spread optimism. Just like you, others prefer to be around people who are not consumed with complaints or worries about imagined awful outcomes. Winston Churchill said it best: "I am an optimist. It does not seem too much use being anything else."

- Start now by giving up complaining. (Requests, yes, complaints, no... this is not about suffering in silence.) Catch yourself complaining and write it down as a problem to solve, a request to make, or a thought to throw out the window.

This is not about *trying hard* to touch others or to make them feel connected. No one wants to feel patronized or manipulated. The key is that if you are successfully living out of the Cornerstone Choices to Love Yourself and Be Yourself, you will be Helping Others to Feel Alive and Connected, just by being around them.

10 READING

For most of us, school-assigned reading is behind us. But LEARNING is never "all done." It can be new and exciting territory to be in charge of deciding what you want to learn next, what book calls to you, and what personal creative outlets you have an inner fire burning to pursue. Choose to be a lifelong learner! For me, I can't get enough of reading the wise words of those who offer their perspectives on "ultimate questions" and life.

"He that loves reading has everything within his reach."

—William Godwin

While I do not consider myself a mystic and I am a lifelong Christian, I find myself loving and appreciating many books in the "guru" genre. These authors do not hesitate to connect spirituality with practical, everyday life. My favorite among them is Sadhguru and I want to share a little bit about him here, in hopes that you will read one or more of his books.

An overview of Sadhguru can be found listed along with his books on Amazon.com: "Sadhguru is a yogi, mystic and visionary. Named one of India's 50 most influential people, Sadhguru's work has touched the lives of millions worldwide through his transformational programs. Sadhguru has a unique ability to make the ancient yogic sciences relevant to contemporary minds. His approach does not ascribe to any belief system but offers methods for self-transformation that are both proven and powerful… Sadhguru has been an influential voice at major global forums including the United Nations and the World Economic Forum, addressing issues as diverse as socioeconomic development, leadership and spirituality.

…Dedicated to the physical, mental and spiritual wellbeing of humanity and gifted with utter clarity of perception, Sadhguru possesses a perspective on life that never fails to intrigue, challenge and surprise all those he encounters. Sadhguru established Isha Foundation, a non-profit, volunteer-run organization operating in more than 300 centers and supported by over 11 million volunteers worldwide. Through powerful yoga programs for inner transformation and inspiring social outreach initiatives, Isha Foundation has created a massive movement dedicated to addressing all aspects of human wellbeing…

In the fall of 2017, Sadhguru initiated Rally For Rivers, a nationwide campaign aiming to implement sustainable and long-term policy changes to revitalize India's severely depleted rivers, which found great support among India's people and leadership. With over 162 Million individuals pledging their support, Rally for Rivers is the largest ecological movement in the world to date."

Sahhguru is one of my favorite teachers and I am so grateful that he has written books for me and others to receive his gifts of wisdom and inspiration.

I am happy to share with you here a few select books by intuitive, loving, influential, smart people. I recommend these books. Each of them is worthwhile. Any of them could turn out to be life-changing for you. All of them have content worth learning.

"The more that you read, the more things you will know. The more that you learn, the more places you'll go."

—Dr. Seuss

RECOMMENDED BOOKS

Bowen, Will (2013). *A Complaint Free World: How to Stop Complaining and Start Enjoying the Life You Always Wanted.* Harmony.

Chamine, Shirzad (2012) *Positive Intelligence: Why Only 20% of Teams and Individuals Achieve Their True Potential and How You Can Achieve Yours.* Greenleaf Book Group Press.

Chopra, Deepak (2021). *Metahuman: Unleashing Your Infinite Potential.* Harmony.

Dee, Barbara (2020). *The Kaizen Method to Living a Healthy Lifestyle.* Suncoast Digital Press.

Lakhiani, Vishen (2020). *The Buddah and the Badass: The Secret Spiritual art of Succeeding at Work.* Rodale Books.

Lakhiami, Vishen (2020). *The Code of the Extraordinary Mind.* Penguin.

Leaf, Dr. Caroline (2021). *Cleaning Up Your Mental Mess: 5 Simple, Scientifically Proven Steps to Reduce Anxiety, Stress, and Toxic Thinking.* Baker Books.

Peale, Norman Vincent (1985). *Have a Great Day: Daily Affirmations for Positive Living.* Open Road Integrated Media.

Peterson, Jordan (2018). *12 Rules for Life: An Antidote to Chaos.* Random House.

Sadhguru (2021). *Karma: A Yogi's Guide to Crafting Your Destiny.* Harmony.

Sharma, Robin (2021). *The Everyday Hero Manifesto: Activate Your Positivity, Maximize Your Productivity, Serve The World.* HarperCollins.

Sharma, Robin (2020). *The 5 AM Club: Own Your Morning, Elevate Your Life.* HarperCollins.

Michael A. Singer (2020) *Untethered Soul: The Journey Beyond Yourself.* Noetic Books.

Tolle, Eckhart (1999) *The Power of Now.* Yogi Impressions.

Zondervan (2019) *NIV, Life Application Study Bible, Third Edition.* Zondervan.

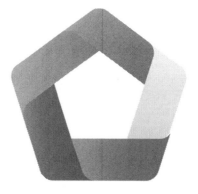

ACKNOWLEDGMENTS

I want to express my thanks and gratitude to all those who have made this book possible. First, Barbara Dee; without her encouragement and help, I could not have completed this project. Her team at Suncoast Digital Press provided high-level expertise, including the creative integration of my principles and my life story.

Second, I would like to thank my always-supportive family, especially my wife, Sheri, and my daughter, Ashley; they have been an absolute cornerstone of support, firmness, honesty, practical help, patience, and planning during the past years of creating this book. Their support did not waver during anything and everything else that has happened in our lives, no matter how urgent or essential.

And third, thank you Costco family, for your love and support during my eight years of partnership. No telling of my life story would be complete without recounting my experiences with this phenomenal organization. I could have written many chapters but only covered the highlights, each a life-changing and fantastic experience.

If you enjoyed this book, please leave a review on Amazon.com.
Thank you!

To contact the author, email: Waleed.Y.Soro@gmail.com

Made in the USA
Columbia, SC
17 August 2022

65223819R00078